THE Power OF Charm

THE Power OF Charm

How to Win Anyone Over in Any Situation

Brian Tracy and Ron Arden

ᴀMACOM

American Management Association

New York • Atlanta • Brussels • Chicago • Mexico City • San Francisco
Shanghai • Tokyo • Toronto • Washington, D. C.

Special discounts on bulk quantities of AMACOM books are available to corporations, professional associations, and other organizations. For details, contact Special Sales Department, AMACOM, a division of American Management Association, 1601 Broadway, New York, NY 10019.
Tel.: 212-903-8316. Fax: 212-903-8083.
Website: www.amacombooks.org

Library of Congress Cataloging-in-Publication Data

Tracy, Brian.
  The power of charm : how to win anyone over in any situation / Brian Tracy and Ron Arden.—1st ed.
    p. cm.
  Includes index.
  ISBN: 0-8144-7357-1
  ISBN: 978-0-8144-7357-3
  1. Interpersonal relations—Handbooks, manuals, etc. 2. Interpersonal communication—Handbooks, manuals, etc. 3. Charm. I. Arden, Ron. II. Title.

  HM1106.T73 2006
  646.7'6–dc22

                        2005033866

Printing number

10 9

We dedicate this book to our wonderful wives,
Nicky and Barbara, the two finest women
in the world, without whose patient
listening we could never have become so
successful at speaking. You are the
most charming women of all.

Contents

Introduction		1
CHAPTER 1	What Is Charm?	3
CHAPTER 2	Charm in Action	5
CHAPTER 3	What Charm Can Do	8
CHAPTER 4	How to Charm Anyone	11
CHAPTER 5	The Magic of Listening	16
CHAPTER 6	Charming a Woman	22
CHAPTER 7	Charming a Man	26
CHAPTER 8	Charming from the Inside Out and from the Outside In	30
CHAPTER 9	The Power of Attention	35
CHAPTER 10	The First Signal: Eye Contact	38
CHAPTER 11	The Second Signal: The Flick	41
CHAPTER 12	The Third Signal: Head Tilts	44
CHAPTER 13	The Fourth Signal: Head Nods	47
CHAPTER 14	The Fifth Signal: Whole Body Language	50
CHAPTER 15	The Sixth Signal: Body Language to Avoid	54
CHAPTER 16	The Seventh Signal: Vocal Reassurances	59
CHAPTER 17	The Eighth Signal: Verbal Reassurances	61
CHAPTER 18	Practice Being Charming with Friends	63

CHAPTER 19 Be Careful with Advice   67

CHAPTER 20 The Power of Patient Listening   70

CHAPTER 21 Be Quick to Smile and Laugh   72

CHAPTER 22 Be Quick to Praise   75

CHAPTER 23 Use the "Act as If" Principle   78

CHAPTER 24 What You Say and How You Say It   83

CHAPTER 25 The Look-Aside   86

CHAPTER 26 The Art of Speaking Slowly   88

CHAPTER 27 The Eloquence of Silence   92

CHAPTER 28 Excessive Fillers Are Charm Killers   95

CHAPTER 29 Charming People with Your Voice   97

CHAPTER 30 Be a Charming Conversationalist   101

CHAPTER 31 Steer the Conversation   104

CHAPTER 32 Do Your Homework   107

CHAPTER 33 Keep the Ball in Their Court   112

CHAPTER 34 Don't "Kill the Ball"   115

CHAPTER 35 Get in Step with the Other Person   118

CHAPTER 36 Practice Makes Perfect   121

CHAPTER 37 Translate Skill into Art   123

CHAPTER 38 Now You Have to Do It!   125

CHAPTER 39 Roll Out the Charm   127

SPECIAL BONUS SECTION:
            The Power of Charm on the Telephone   129

Index   137

About the Authors   143

THE Power OF Charm

Introduction

You must have this charm to reach the pinnacle. It is made of everything and of nothing, the striving will, the look, the walk, the proportions of the body, the sound of the voice, the ease of the gestures. It is not at all necessary to be handsome or to be pretty; all that is needful is charm.

—SARAH BERNHARDT

Fully 85 percent of your success in business and personal life will be determined by your ability to communicate effectively with others. "Social intelligence," or the ability to interact, converse, negotiate with, and persuade others, is the most highly paid and respected form of intelligence you can have, and this intelligence can be developed.

You can learn to be a warm, friendly, likable, and *charming* individual just by practicing some of the communication methods and techniques used by the most influential and effective people in our world today.

The "secrets" of great communicators are not secrets at

1

all. They are simply proven methods of interacting with others in a way that makes them open to you and receptive to your message. As a result, they are more willing to be influenced by you, to buy from you, to enter into business and personal relationships with you, and to think of you in positive terms.

Your ability to be charming, to be a genuinely likable and pleasant person, will likely open more doors for you than any other quality. The more people like you and think of you warmly, the more they will want to see you, listen to you, be in your presence, and invite you into theirs.

In the hundreds of speeches we've given and to the thousands of people we've trained, we have repeatedly said, "The most valuable commodity in the world isn't gold or diamonds—it's charm." Your reputation, how people think and talk about you when you are not there, is your most valuable personal and professional asset. It is the sum total of the impression you make on others when they spend time in your presence.

By learning the simple truths about charm and practicing the techniques that follow, you can dramatically improve the effectiveness and enjoyment of your interactions with all others, starting with your family and extending to everyone you meet.

You will be more successful, earn more money, get promoted faster, make more sales, prevail in more negotiations, and be more persuasive and influential with everyone you meet.

CHAPTER 1

What Is Charm?

When John F. Kennedy flashed his smile,
he could charm a bird off a tree.

—SEYMOUR ST. JOHN

Listen to the description of charm by someone who did not expect it and may have been resistant to its effect before succumbing:

> ... [H]e projected a totally 'in the moment' focus on each person he met.... [H]e exuded warmth; he seemed a man genuinely interested in liking you, and not concerned with whether or not you liked him. How much of that was genetic and how much developed I can only speculate. All I know is that I was, in that brief moment of meeting, totally charmed by a person I neither agreed with nor even expected to like.

These remarks are by professional speaker Mark Sanborn, commenting on meeting President Bill Clinton.

When we refer to charm, we're not talking about table manners, good looks, or being a snappy dresser; we're talking about something much more profound. True charm is something that goes beyond mere appearance. It's that ability some people have to create extraordinary rapport that makes others in their presence feel exceptional. Charm has an engaging quality to which we respond powerfully and emotionally, almost instinctively.

Nature or Nurture?

You might be saying to yourself, "But you have to be born with charm, and if you're not, you're out of luck!" We used to believe that too, but in all the many years that we have researched, experimented with, and taught the art and craft of person-to-person communication, we have found much evidence to the contrary.

There's no question that some people are naturally charming, which gives them an advantage. But charm is not some mystical ingredient that is found in our genes. Charm is the result of using specific skills that most of us know little or nothing about. This means charm can be learned.

In the pages ahead, you will learn how to become a completely charismatic person, exerting a magnetic attraction and influence on the people you meet.

Your Tools for Charming Others

From now on, think about charm as a personality quality and skill you can develop by doing the things that charming people do and being the kind of person that charming people are.

CHAPTER 2

Charm in Action

Charm: A quality that exerts an irresistible
power to please and attract.

—THE DICTIONARY

R on Arden relates this personal story as a testament
to the power of charm:

It was back in the seventies that my awareness of the
power of charm really took root. A friend of ours in Los
Angeles phoned to invite my wife Nicky and me to a recep-
tion for Ivan Berold and his wife Maryanne. They had
recently arrived here from South Africa. Ivan, a handsome
devil and a good actor and friend, is someone I had known
during my theater days in South Africa.

We arrived at their home that Saturday afternoon and

joined the crowd in the garden. People were milling around the bar and, of course, Ivan and Maryanne. We greeted each other warmly and then the four of us proceeded to "fill up" at the inviting buffet tables.

Later that afternoon I saw Nicky and Ivan talking to each other, and I noticed that my dear, normally level-headed wife seemed entranced by him. I thought, "What on earth is going on? She's behaving like a teenybopper." An irrational pang of jealousy shot through me and I hurried over to join them.

The Power of Fascination

Soon after, I said to Nicky, "What is so fascinating about Ivan that you looked mesmerized by him?"

She thought for a moment and said, "When he speaks to you, it's as though you're in a cocoon with him. No one exists in the world for him but you. And when he listens, he listens as though every word you say is important and needs his undivided attention."

When I thought about it, I realized she was absolutely right. Ever since I've known him, he has displayed that same quality when he's with anyone. He radiates charm continuously. That's why Ivan is very much a lady's man and very much a man's man, too.

A Lifelong Interest Leads to These Simple Rules

Though this event happened more than twenty years ago, I remember it like it was yesterday. As my dear wife reminds me, my first deep interest in charm seemed to happen about then.

And my interest grew. I set about studying and identifying the behaviors that all people of charm use. I questioned many of these individuals to get an idea of how they feel about their impact on others. One of the fascinating things I discovered was that those who charm get great pleasure in giving others pleasure.

I set about reducing what I had learned into identifiable and manageable lessons, each lesson having its own set of simple rules and techniques that are easy to understand and just as easy to learn and to do.

Brian Tracy and I have successfully trained many others to use these skills, whether for professional or social reasons, and now you, too, can learn how to control the dynamics of your own impact on people. Once you discover how to wield the power of charm, you'll have at your disposal one of the most valuable elements for success—how to make people feel like a million.

Your Tools for Charming Others

Think of the most charming person you know. Observe the person's behavior. Try to identify what he does when being charming. Watch the effect it has on others and use what you observe and learn as motivation to become, in your own way, just like your model—charming, persuasive, and admirable.

What Charm
Can Do

Charm is captivating. Just as the petals of a flower unfold and open to the warmth and light of the sun, so do we unfold and open to the enchantment of charm. Charm acts as the Great Attractor, drawing us toward its magnetic source.
—THOKOZA, A 20TH CENTURY WISE WOMAN

Those who have charm usually get listened to and often get extra chances. They are given opportunities others may never get. They can be forgiven for things others would be crucified for. They will be told things that others may never hear. People make excuses for them, go out of their way for them, and always give them the benefit of the doubt. Let's face it, you probably know someone who has reached you in a very compelling and profound fashion. If so, you've been on the receiving end of someone's charm offensive.

Feeling Like a Million

At some time or another, we've all met someone who has the talent to sweep you away with their charm. They seemed to truly like you. They valued your opinion. They devoted all of their attention to you and nobody else. When they were with you, no one but you existed for them, no matter who else was around. They made you feel as though you were the most fascinating and important person they'd ever met. You totally suspended critical judgment for the pleasure of their company. Do you remember how wonderful you felt? I bet you felt like a million.

Think what *power* there is in being able to make somebody feel wonderful about himself. It's unlimited! Great political leaders nurture it, successful businesspeople cultivate it, and famous entertainers exploit it. Nearly everyone who deals with people can benefit from charm, and anyone wanting to climb the ladder to success should develop it.

Anytime? Anywhere?

What if you were able to create that special feeling for others anytime, anywhere? How valuable do you think that gift might be in your personal life and your business world? Absolutely priceless, believe me. When you have the power to make people feel special, the rewards are usually close behind.

Your Tools for Charming Others

Decide today that you are going to develop the power of charm and practice it in your relationships with others. This decision will open you to all the things you can do to make other people feel wonderful about themselves.

Measure your current "charm quotient." Give yourself a grade from one to ten on how charming you believe you are already, with ten being "excellent." Then ask someone you know to grade you as well. Whatever number that person assigns to you is the *true* measure.

Now you are ready to begin transforming yourself into a genuinely and powerfully charming person.

CHAPTER 4

How to Charm Anyone

They don't care how much you know until they know how much you care.

—LOU HOLTZ

Psychologists tell us that the core of personality is self-esteem. This has best been defined as *"how much you like yourself."* Your self-esteem is the sum total of how important and valuable you feel you are at any moment.

Human beings are intensely emotional. They make decisions emotionally and then justify them logically. People are powerfully affected by their emotional environment, especially the behavior of other people toward them.

From infancy, you are conditioned to be hypersensitive to the actions and reactions of your parents toward you. Often, the dynamics of these early exchanges set you up for life in your relationships with others. Almost everything you do involving others is either to bolster your self-esteem, your inner sense of well-being, or to protect it from being diminished by other people or circumstances.

The Secret of Charm

The deepest craving of human nature is the need to feel valued and valuable. The secret of charm is therefore simple: *make others feel important.*

Five Ways to Be Charming

The more important you make people feel in your presence, the more charming they will perceive you to be. Fortunately, we know how to make people feel wonderful about themselves. These key behaviors can be summarized in the five As: acceptance, appreciation, approval, admiration, and attention.

   1. *Acceptance.* The greatest gift that you can give other people is the attitude of "unconditional positive regard." That is, you accept them in their entirety, without limitation. You never criticize or find fault. You are totally accepting of everything about them, as if they were a miracle of nature. This is the starting point of being charming.

   And how do you express complete acceptance? It is simple. You smile! When you smile with happiness at seeing people, their self-esteem jumps automatically. They feel happy about themselves. They feel important and valuable. And they like the person who is making them feel this way. They find you to be charming, even before you open your mouth.

2. *Appreciation.* Whenever you express appreciation to others for something they have done, small or large, their self-esteem increases. They feel more valuable and important. They feel more competent and capable. Their self-image improves and their self-respect soars.

And how do you trigger this wonderful feeing in others? It is simple. You say "thank you" on every occasion, for any large or small reason. You make a habit of thanking everyone in your world for everything they do. Thank your secretary for her work. Thank your spouse for his help. Thank your children for anything they do that you appreciate.

Here is the double payoff: Whenever you smile or say thank you to another person, not only does that person's self-esteem and feeling of importance jump, but so does *yours.* You actually like yourself more every time you do or say anything that causes other people to like themselves more.

And the more you like yourself, the more you will genuinely like and care about others. The more you like yourself, the less concerned you will be about whether you are making a good impression, and the more naturally charming you will become.

3. *Approval.* It is said that "babies cry for it, men die for it." Throughout life, all humans have a deep subconscious need for approval of their actions and accomplishments. No amount of approval ever satisfies for long. The need is ongoing, like the need for food and rest. People who continually seek opportunities to express approval are welcome wherever they go.

Perhaps the best definition of approval is "praise." This subject is so important that we will come back to it later. Just remember, whenever you praise other people for something they have done, their self-esteem is elevated. They feel wonderful about themselves. And they find you to be more interesting, perceptive, highly likable, and extremely charming.

4. *Admiration.* As Abraham Lincoln said, "Everybody likes a compliment." When you give people a genuine, sincere compliment about a trait, possession, or accomplishment, they automatically feel better about themselves. They feel acknowledged and recognized. They feel valuable and important. They like themselves more, and they like you more.

Compliment a person on an article of clothing. Compliment someone on a trait, like punctuality or persistence. Compliment the person on having won an award or achieved a goal. Compliment for small things as well as large. Always be looking for something to compliment, and each time you find something, the other person will like you more and find you to be charming.

5. *Attention.* This is perhaps the most important quality of all, and will be the subject of several subsequent chapters. It is the most powerful behavior for building self-esteem and is the key to instant charm. When you pay close attention to other people, the more valuable and important they will feel they are, and the more they will like you.

These are the five most powerful self-esteem building tools ever discovered. As you master them through practice, you will become one of the most charming and influential people in your social and professional circle.

Your Tools for Charming Others

The next time you meet your significant other or even someone you work with, conduct this exercise: Imagine that when you were young, you had a dear friend with whom you shared many of the important emotional experiences of your young life. But years passed and you lost touch. You had no idea where your friend had gone.

One day, when you are walking down the street, or maybe you are at a social function, suddenly there he is! You are shocked, amazed, overwhelmed with a flood of memories and affection. Your whole face lights up and all you can think is, "It's *you!*"

Wow! You are so happy to see this person. You feel excited and delighted and grateful and emotional all at the same time.

Now, the next time you meet a person or persons who are important to you, especially loved ones or dear friends, create this same feeling and act as if you are rediscovering them after a too-long absence, as if you were declaring, "There you *are!*" Treat these special people as if seeing them makes you incredibly happy. Smile and beam at them. Focus all your attention on them. Treat them as if they were the most important person in the world at this moment. No matter who they are, they will think that you are an incredibly charming person.

CHAPTER 5

The Magic of Listening

Rapt attention is the highest form of flattery.

—DALE CARNEGIE

Your ability to listen well in a social or business conversation can help you as much as any other skill you develop. One of the most important qualities of a leader is the ability to gather information by asking questions and listening closely to what people have to say.

Daniel Goleman, author of *Emotional Intelligence*, concluded that your ability to connect emotionally with people, your EQ, is as vital to your success, and perhaps even more so, than your IQ. He defined the most important quality of EQ as "empathy," or the ability to be aware of and sensitive to what people say and what they really mean.

Howard Gardner of Harvard University has defined this quality as "social intelligence," which, as we noted at the outset of this book, is the highest paid and most respected form of intelligence in our society. And fortunately, it can be learned just by becoming a good listener.

Four Keys to Effective Listening

Every book, article, or course on this subject ultimately comes to the same conclusion: There are four key elements of effective listening. If you can master them, your "charm quotient" will skyrocket immediately.

1. *Listen attentively.* Listen without interrupting. Listen in complete silence, as if there is nothing in the world that is more important to you at this moment than what the other person is saying.

If someone wants to talk to you, especially at home, immediately discontinue all other activities and give that person your complete attention.

Turn off the television, shut the book or newspaper, and focus single-mindedly on what the other person is saying. This behavior will be instantly recognized and appreciated, and will give you tremendous emotional power in the conversation.

To listen as if you are transfixed by what the other person is saying, imagine that your eyes are sunlamps and you are giving the person's face a tan.

When a person is intently listened to by another, he is affected biochemically. His brain releases endorphins, nature's "happy drug," which makes him feel good about himself. His self-esteem goes up and he likes himself more. Above all, he likes and trusts you more by virtue of your listening attentively to him. The payoff is extraordinary.

2. *Pause before replying.* Rather than jumping in as soon as the other person takes a breath, pause for three to five seconds. Allow a silence to exist. Just relax.

When you pause, three things happen, all of them good. First, you avoid interrupting the other person if he is just pausing to reorganize his thoughts before continuing. Second, by pausing, you tell the person that what he said was important and that you are considering it carefully. This reinforces the personal value of the speaker and causes him to see you as a more attractive and intelligent person. Third, you actually *hear* the person, not only what he said, but what he meant, at a deeper level of mind. Try it once and see.

3. *Question for clarification.* Never assume that you know exactly what the person meant by what he said. Instead, help him to expand on his most recent remark by asking, "How do you mean?" or "What do you mean, exactly?"

Here is one of the most important rules of communication: *The person who asks questions has control.*

The person answering the questions is controlled by the person asking them. When a person is speaking in answer to a question, fully 100 percent of his focus and attention is on what he is saying; he cannot think of anything else. He is totally controlled by the questioner.

The trick to charming someone with this technique is to ask your questions thoughtfully. All great communicators know this and use it regularly.

4. *Feed it back; paraphrase it in your own words.* This is the acid test of effective listening, the proof that you were really paying attention, instead of engaging in the "phony listening" that is so common today.

When a person finishes speaking, you pause and say something like, "So, you just did this, and then this happened, and then you decided to do that, right?"

Only when the speaker confirms that's what he said and meant do you continue, either by asking another question or commenting on what has just been said.

Why Women Are Wonderful Listeners

In general, women are excellent listeners already. When a woman communicates, according to MRI scans, fully *seven* centers of her brain are involved. In men, it is only *two*.

Men often listen halfheartedly to women, especially if the television is on. That's because men can only process one sensory input at a time. They cannot, for example, both watch television and listen to someone else speaking, which women can do much more easily.

The worst sin a man can commit with the woman in his life is not to listen to her when she is speaking. Every man has heard the woman accuse, angrily, *"You're not listening to me!"*

The typical male response is to quickly say, "Yes, I am."

Then she has you. She folds her arms and asks demandingly, *"All right, then. What did I just say?"*

It is only if he can feed it back to her with some accuracy that she knows for sure that he was really listening.

For you to become a completely charming person, you must learn to master the techniques of listening—especially if you are a man. Developing this key skill will take discipline and determination at first, but it will become easy and automatic over time.

Listening with a Difference

Effective listening means listening with a *difference*. It's not the "lend me your ear and I'll tell you a story" type of listening; rather, it's about convincing people you are totally involved in what is being said.

Ron on Charming People by Listening to Them

I remember once watching a friend of mine who was the hostess of a party. She was chatting with great animation to someone unfamiliar to me. When he left, she crossed over to me and said, "Do you know Roger Pitt, that delightful man I was just talking to?" I didn't. "Well, he's one of the most charming people I've ever met, and what a great conversationalist—intelligent, articulate, and amusing—you must meet him!"

Inwardly I smiled. *"A great conversationalist, intelligent, articulate, and amusing,"* she said. Well, while I was watching, he rarely seemed to utter more than a word or two—but he was, I noticed, a great listener. And in so being, he absolutely charmed his hostess.

Your Tools for Charming Others

Try these effective listening techniques—listening, pausing, asking thoughtful questions, and paraphrasing—one at a time. Begin by practicing attentive listening at home and at work. Make no attempt to interrupt. Just hang on the other person's every word.

Practice controlling and directing the conversation by using these various techniques. You'll discover you can communicate more deeply with a person in a few minutes by asking questions and listening closely to the answers than you could in several weeks by talking all the time.

CHAPTER 6

Charming a Woman

If God made anything better than a girl, Dover thought,
He sure kept it to himself.
—NELSON ALGREN, *A Walk on the Wild Side*

Men and women are different, in ways other than the obvious.

One of the most important applications of charm is to be sensitive and attractive to the women in your world. Women love men who are charming. They want to be with them constantly.

To be charming to women, you have to understand how they think and feel. You must then say and do the things that affect them emotionally if you want them to like you.

Most women's primary source of personal value and self-esteem comes from the quality of their relationships with the important people in their lives. They place an even higher emphasis than men on outward appearance and on how well they are perceived and treated by others.

Three Deep Needs of Every Woman

The most powerful and important emotional needs of most women are *affection, attention, and respect.* They judge other people by their caring and concern for them, and by their confidence and competence in the world. They can see past external appearances and look into the heart of the person they are talking to.

The way to charm a woman is by being totally, 100 percent captivated by her as a person, and by every word she says, without interrupting or stopping her flow of conversation. Just as two young people in love sit and look into each other's eyes, so should you allow yourself to be completely, totally fascinated by the woman you are talking to and whom you want to charm.

Talk Less, Listen More

A comedienne once said, "I love going to my therapist. I get to talk nonstop about myself for an hour, just like a man on a first date." This is all too true.

Instead, the next time you are with a woman you care about, resist the overwhelming temptation to talk about yourself as if your day was the most fascinating event since Jesus walked the earth. Rather, ask her questions about herself and her day, about her life and her concerns, and then listen quietly and attentively to the answers. She will find you to be charming.

> ### Brian on Listening and Questioning
>
> Some years ago, when I was a bachelor, I took an attractive young woman out to dinner. Throughout the dinner, I asked her questions about herself. At a certain point, she opened up and told me about a particularly sad thing that had happened to her.
>
> I was so moved by her pain at recalling the event that I winced. "I'm so sorry that happened to you," I said. And I really meant it. We sat there silently for a couple of minutes while I held her hand and allowed her to just relax in my presence, with no comment.
>
> It was the beginning of a fulfilling relationship. My genuine concern for her feelings and her experience created a powerful bond between us.

To Impress or to Be Impressed?

When you are with a woman you want to charm, instead of talking about yourself and trying to impress her, be impressed *by* her. Ask her questions and talk to her about her hopes and concerns, her background, her goals and desires. Talk and listen as if you find her to be the most fascinating person you ever met.

The more you are impressed by her, by her ideas and opinions, her character and personality, the more impressed she will be with you. She will find you to be absolutely charming.

Your Tools for Charming Others

Select a woman in your life, at work or at home, and imagine that she is the most interesting and fascinating person you have ever met. Treat her with extreme courtesy and respect. Hang on her every word. Ask questions and listen closely to the answers. See how long you can encourage her to speak without interrupting or talking about yourself.

The next time you meet a woman you like, practice the same skills of *acceptance, appreciation, and approval.* Ask her about her work and personal life, and find something to be impressed about, or even to be amazed by. The wonder of these behaviors is that the more you practice them, the more interesting and fascinating you will truly find her to be. And she will think of you as being unusually charming.

CHAPTER 7

Charming a Man

There are three classes of men—lovers of wisdom, lovers of honor, lovers of gain.

—PLATO

Men are suckers for charm, like putty in your hands. From long experience, women are often suspicious of a man who is trying to be charming, knowing that he, being a man, may have ulterior motives. Men, on the other hand, are much more open to being charmed, if you do it right.

Men get their greatest sense of value and importance from achievement, status, and the respect of the key people in their worlds. Men are driven and motivated to bring home the bacon and provide for themselves and their families. This is central to their self-image and identity. Some men can never rest. No matter how much they have accomplished, they feel insecure; they feel as if they must accomplish more.

Men have what psychologists call "insecurity of status." Many of them have a deep-down, unspoken fear that everything they have accomplished could be taken away from them at any moment. They must continually achieve more and more, no matter what they have accomplished in the past.

The key to charming a man is simple. Ask him questions and appreciate him for his *achievements*. Acknowledge and recognize him for his work and accomplishments. Be impressed with what he is doing and what he has done. He will find you fascinating.

Brian on Praising Accomplishments

When my son Michael was about five, he came home one day from Montessori school with a happy look on his face. I asked him, "How was school today?"

He beamed at me and replied, "My teacher told me that she was really proud of me." He then repeated, as if it was very important, *"She was really proud of me."*

I immediately recognized that the teacher had hit an emotional chord in Michael that I could strike as well. From that day forward, I have continually told my children, *"I am really proud of you,"* whenever they did anything worthwhile. Every time I said these words, I saw how it elevated their self-esteem and sense of personal value.

As a busy professional speaker, I meet thousands of people each year. Whenever someone tells me about something he has accomplished, I say something like, *"You must be very proud of that."* Men, especially, are deeply affected when people they respect tell them how proud they are of some achievement. They find it both moving and charming.

What Men Need

Men are charmed when you appreciate that they are capable of succeeding and providing.

When a woman smiles at a man, it makes him happy, reinforcing his self-esteem and making him feel more secure. Any expression of praise, approval, or admiration for his accomplishments warms his heart and causes him to see you as a remarkably perceptive person.

When a woman lavishes attention on a man as he talks and explains his work and career path, practicing all the listening skills she has learned in this book, he will find her absolutely fascinating.

You often see an ordinary-looking woman with a good-looking, successful man and say, "I wonder what he sees in her?"

The answer is, *"What she sees in him!"* When a woman looks into a man's eyes and sees a valuable and important person, he finds her irresistible. He is absolutely charmed.

Your Tools for Charming Others

Select any man in your life and ask him a simple question like, "How is everything going at work?" When he answers, lean forward and pay close attention, as if his response was absolutely fascinating.

When he slows down or stops speaking, which he will to test whether you are really interested, follow up with one of these questions: "What happened then?" or "What did you do (say) then?" He will almost immediately begin speaking again, which gives you more of an opportunity to listen and appreciate his accomplishments.

CHAPTER 8

Charming from the Inside Out and from the Outside In

The fundamental rule of the Age of Celebrity: It doesn't matter
what you are; it only matters what people think you are.

—LANCE MORROW

Now that you know the basics of charming people, of affecting them at a deep emotional level, let's look at the reasons why charm works so that you can better practice the techniques in this book to become even better at getting your own sweet way.

In the theater, there are two core approaches to acting:

the American approach, which is referred to as "inside out," and the European approach, which is "outside in." Using the American method, actors begin the work of creating a character in a play from a psychological point of view. They search for personal qualities inside themselves that are similar to those of the character. Using those similarities, the actor builds outward, layer upon layer, to create all the attitudes and behaviors of the person he or she will eventually portray. (One drawback of this approach: Actors are forced to spend a great deal of time convincing themselves with no guarantees they will convince others.)

In the self-improvement arena, there are many inside-out equivalents: We are encouraged to look inside ourselves for the sources of our behaviors and understand why we do and say what we do. The belief is that by changing the way we think on the inside, we will change the way we act on the outside. Sometimes it works, sometimes it doesn't.

The European Approach

When building a character using the European approach, actors begin by creating the outward behaviors of the characters they will play. They first imagine the way the characters would walk, talk, and behave. Then the actor moves inward, layer by layer, developing the psychological reasons for the behaviors of the person being played.

This device is also used in the self-improvement arena. By changing our external behaviors we can influence what others feel and also what we feel inside. For instance, if you *behave* as though you are happy or excited you will probably convince others that you are happy and excited; but an added bonus is that you, too, will begin to *feel* happy or excited.

The Power of Charm has been written as an outside-in book. In it, we deal with how you can change your *external* behavior by developing and using certain skills—skills that give you control of the personal image that you want others to see. We let your inner dynamics take care of themselves.

Ron on an Unexpected Transformation

An old friend of ours, let's call her Miriam, came to visit us to apologize for her outburst at dinner a few nights before. Her mood swings and eruptions were legendary. She mentioned that she had been seeing the same psychiatrist for seven years. "*Seven years,*" echoed my wife Nicky. "That's an awfully long time to stay with any shrink."

"Tell me, after all that time, do you think you've got your money's worth?" I asked, which provoked an icy glare from my wife.

"Well," Miriam thought for a moment, "yes and no. I understand why I behave the way I do, but I still can't really control myself. So I've been wondering about that, whether all the time and money has been worth it."

She seemed quite dejected and defeated as she sat there.

Nicky said, "Have you ever thought about changing to another therapist? We know a psychologist who specializes in behavioral problems. Would you be willing to have a chat with him, he might be able to help?"

Miriam was quiet for a while then said, "I may as well"— and she sighed—"*I've nothing to lose.*"

We didn't hear from or see her for some time. Then one evening she called. I answered the phone.

"Hello, Ron, this is Miriam."

"Miriam, how are you?"

"Coming along fine," she replied.

"What happened with the psychologist?" I asked. "Did you ever call him?"

"Yes, I did," she said, "I've been seeing him for a few weeks now and there's already quite a difference. What's interesting is that he really doesn't bother too much about why I do things; he mostly concentrates on how I can behave differently."

We saw Miriam at a dinner party a couple of months later and the change was astonishing. The kind of things that would have had her pounding the table or going *mano a mano* with anyone who contradicted her were now ignored. She was a pleasure to be with.

When we commented on the change, she told us, "It's not only that I can control my behavior no matter what's going on inside me, but I don't get as agitated as I used to. I've learned that changing my behavior reduces my agitation."

Concentrate on Behavior

Miriam's story is a confirmation of the difference between "inside out" and "outside in" as it applied to everyday life. It's a fact: Knowing *why* you're doing things does not automatically mean that you know *how* to change them. If you really want change, worry less about the why and concentrate more on the how. It is often easier and faster for us to change from the outside than to change from the inside.

Behavior Is Everything

To go back to the example at the beginning of Chapter 1, do you think that Bill Clinton was genuinely interested in Mark Sanborn, or was his warmth, his utter "in the moment" focus, a cultivated behavior? And does it really matter? Regardless of what's going on in your head, what you are ultimately judged by is your *behavior.* If you behave as though you hate, then you hate; if you behave as though you love, then you love; if you behave as though you care, you care.

People will react based on how they *perceive* us to behave, no matter what our inner agendas may be.

Your Tools for Charming Others

Don't worry so much about changing the way you think and feel inside, because it may take a long time to show any improvement or results. Instead, concentrate on behaving exactly as if you were *already* a charming person. Create a mental image of yourself as absolutely charming on the inside, and then act accordingly on the outside.

Select someone you feel is already charming and think about how that person treats others in conversation. Try to do the same things that person does when you talk to others.

The Power of Attention

Our companions please us less from the charms we find in their conversation than from those they find in ours.

—FULKE GREVILLE

Here is a scenario that I'm sure is familiar to most everyone, particularly at the breakfast or dinner table. It sounds something like this:

She: "You aren't listening to me!"

He: "Yes I am!"

She: "No you're not!"

He: "I tell you I am!"

She: "I'm telling you you're not!"

He: "I am. I can repeat every damn word you said!"

She: "I don't give a damn if you can. You aren't listen-
      ing to me!

What she is really telling him is that even if he has 100
percent recall, he is failing to convince her that he is giving
her his undivided attention.

Undivided Attention

Charm requires undivided attention—especially when listening. Unless you're at a lecture, remembering what
someone says is only a part of listening. If your attitude
seems to be saying, "I don't care enough to bother to react
to you"—if nothing in your behavior confirms you are listening—you are being a lousy listener. If there aren't any
signals coming from you that say you're paying attention
… you aren't listening!

Good relationships, whether social or professional, are
built on many qualities, but nothing is as important as
being perceived as being an empathetic listener. The better
listener you are, the more valuable you are in any relationship. But how do we know if somebody is listening with
complete attention?

You do what great listeners do—you signal that you are
listening. Your behavior and body language should say, "I
am totally focused on what you are saying; every word you
utter is of extreme importance to me."

Those who send this signal are termed "attentive listeners." Those who don't are called "inattentive listeners."

Give Acknowledgments and Assurances

We refer to these signals as "acknowledgments and reassurances." Attentive listeners use them to *acknowledge* the other person's presence and *reassure* them they are totally involved in the act of listening. Attentive listeners project that "in the moment" focus that makes people feel special and important. The more of these signals you practice, the more charming you will appear.

Your Tools for Charming Others

The next time you are conversing with someone, make a special effort to acknowledge and reassure that person that you are fully engaged in the conversation and involved in what he is saying. Face the person directly and concentrate on his words. Act as if this is the last time you will ever see him. Learn how to signal to the person that you are paying attention.

CHAPTER 10

The First Signal: Eye Contact

An ounce of dialogue is worth a pound of monologue.

—ANONYMOUS

How do you know when someone is listening to you? The first important signal is eye contact, pure and simple. If someone is not looking at you, that person is not listening to you.

How many times have you thought, or perhaps said, particularly to your children, *"Will you look at me when I'm talking to you!"* Do you know how irritating it is when people don't look at you when you are talking to them, and how much more comfortable you feel when they do?

Brian's Recommended Experiment

Here is a little experiment you can do to illustrate how important eye contact is in communicating with another person. Start off by looking straight at the person to whom you are talking, or who is talking to you. Then slowly allow your gaze to drift away into the distance, no longer looking at the person who is talking.

The reaction will be almost immediate, as if you just pulled the verbal carpet out from under him. He will stop talking in the middle of a sentence as soon as you stop looking at him. It happens every time.

Ron on the Perils of Losing Eye Contact

In my early acting days, as part of my training I had a fencing instructor—Stanley Coghan. He was a fine teacher and a modest, rather quiet man. But when he put on his teaching hat he was a terror. Woe betide you if you allowed your eyes to stray when he was correcting or demonstrating a parry or thrust. With fingers seemingly attached to wire hawsers in his bulging forearm, he would abruptly take your jaw in his grasp. And while the bones in your jaw seemed to be cracking under the pressure, he would slowly turn your head toward him and gently say, *"Look at me when I'm speaking to you— please!"* I promise you, after a couple of those reminders, I always did.

Look Directly at the Speaker

Make direct eye contact. That's the basic way people will know if you're listening. The more eye contact you give, the more involved you seem.

How much eye contact is right? When you are listening, there is no such thing as too much: Ideally, it should be a hundred percent. If you look away too often or for too long, you will almost certainly trigger negative reactions in the other person, who will begin to think, "I'm boring, he doesn't like me," or "She's not interested in what I have to say."

Not one positive thought is created by poor eye contact. For you to be perceived as charming, you must practice excellent eye contact when you are listening.

Your Tools for Charming Others

In your next conversation, practice staying "in the moment." When you want to be charming, you must "be there." Whether you spend a minute or an hour with the other person, discipline yourself to remain totally focused on the now. You can't be charming if you're not there.

Resolve to develop the habit of using direct eye contact when you are listening. Select a social or business occasion when people are speaking to you. As they are speaking, make sure that your eyes are looking into their eyes, not the bridges of their noses, their foreheads, or beyond their left ears. Focus your attention. Try not to allow any distractions. Don't be tempted to scout the room looking for more important or desirable company. Don't eye the bar or food table. Allow your eyes and your attention to belong to them until they finish speaking.

Practice the technique of focused eye contact at home with your family as well. Once you find yourself paying close attention to others naturally and easily, you may then move from good eye contact to *superior* eye contact—always a "must" for the skilled charmer. This brings us to Chapter 11 on "the flick."

The Second Signal: The Flick

*The reason why we have two ears and only one mouth is that
we may listen the more and talk the less.*

—ZENO OF ATHENS, 350 B.C.

When you are listening, *superior* eye contact requires an additional skill that increases the naturalness of your eye contact. It also helps to avoid the possibility of intimidation that intense eye contact can produce. Additionally, it suggests the depth of your involvement with the person and in what she or he is saying. It is called "the flick."

What is the flick? Flicking is the simple act of shifting

your gaze from one of the person's eyes to the other while you are listening. If you want to see the flick in action, the next time you're watching television and there's a love scene where the young girl is looking into the young man's eyes, turn down the sound. As she gazes into his eyes, watch how her eyes flick from his one eye to the other. He will do the same. She will even create a triangle of flicks between his eyes and lips, making her eye contact very intimate and very sensual. Their eye movement mutually tells them how much their minds and feelings are actively engaged with each other.

Genuine Listening versus Phony Listening

You have probably experienced the reverse of this total engagement. Someone has been looking at you and very possibly making a hundred percent eye contact, but you knew "the lights were on but there was no one home." The other person was engaging in phony listening. He wasn't listening to you. His eyes had that glazed, vacant look, which immediately confirmed your worst suspicion—he wasn't really interested in you or what you had to say.

What caused that vacant look? It's the lack of eye *activity*. The person's eyes seemed to be locked in one place— just staring at you. And the longer he just sat there, the more uncomfortable and even angry you felt.

Move Your Eyes

If you want people to *see* that you are listening, your eyes must move. Just like you saw on TV, the more eye activity there is, the more you will appear to be involved. The less eye activity, the less you will appear involved, and where there is no eye activity, there will seem to be no involvement at all.

A perfect example of "no activity, no involvement" was the presidential candidate and political gadfly, Ross Perot. Whenever you saw him on TV, either when he was speaking or listening, he rarely moved his eyes: He never seemed to blink. He just stared. This glaring absence of eye activity indicated he wasn't considering any other opinions; he wasn't weighing the value or merit of what was being said: His mind was made up. He was interested only in what he was going to say next.

Your Tools for Charming Others

Once you have mastered the art of prolonged eye contact, begin at home to practice and learn the technique of flicking. The next time you're listening to someone, concentrate on shifting your eyes back and forth between their eyes every now and then. Don't overdo it. You don't want to appear as though you've developed a tic! After some practice, you will quickly find you don't have to try to flick—it will just happen by itself.

If you are concerned about how often you should flick, just watch someone who is a really good, attentive listener. Observe people when they are engaged in two-way conversations at work, at social engagements, or even on TV. The way they use their eyes will give you a good sense of what is appropriate.

Eye flicks are one of the best signals that tell a speaker that she has captured your interest. Now let us look at another way to express charm.

CHAPTER 12

The Third Signal: Head Tilts

Self confidence adds more to conversation than wit.
—LA ROCHEFOUCAULD

The motions you make with your body and head exert an inordinate influence on other people.

Even Dogs Know This Trick

If you have a dog, you probably sometimes feel that he is listening to you and that he understands you. That is why they say that a dog is man's best friend. There is a valuable lesson to be learned from your dog.

Ron on How to Look Inquisitive

Many years ago, unbeknown to me, my wife Nicky brought home a young puppy. She hadn't meant to ignore me in making this decision on her own, but had fallen in love with the dog. When I arrived home that evening, *bingo*, there she was, a very cute, very spotted Dalmatian puppy. Cute! I knelt down to say hello just at the moment she jumped up to say hello. There was an immediate and painful collision between her muzzle and my muzzle. The result: a broken lip—my lip. But regardless of our first meeting, as the days, weeks, and months went by, Pepper became the love of both our lives.

We often talked to her as though she could understand. And when we spoke, Pepper would always tilt her head this way and that. She looked for all the world as though she could understand our every word. Now, common sense tells us that that is impossible, but she sure *looked* as though she knew what we were saying!

If you do the same and occasionally tilt your head slightly to one side as you listen to someone tell you something, it will give you a more intense, inquiring look. It's as though you are screwing your focus more tightly on the speaker. If you use this technique when the speaker is talking about something she thinks is significant, you will look very attentive and involved. She will find this little gesture of yours very charming.

Your Tools for Charming Others

The next time someone is talking to you, especially when it is about something that is important to her, try a small tilt of your head to either side. You might even practice in front of a mirror before you try it on a person, just to see how it looks.

Here's another rule: Tilt your head to listen, straighten up to speak.

Then practice combining all three of the methods you've learned thus far: Use direct eye contact with each person in every conversation, flick your gaze from eye to eye, and tilt your head to the left or right when someone is speaking to you.

They are all part of the system of signals that great listeners use to say, *"I am totally focused on what you're saying."* They are small but very powerful indicators of the depth of your listening and the degree of your involvement in a conversation.

The Fourth Signal: Head Nods

That is the happiest conversation where there is no competition,
no vanity, but a calm quiet interchange of sentiments.

—SAMUEL JOHNSON

H ead nodding is another powerful technique in listening and appearing charming to others. Some people tend to nod instinctively; some don't nod very much at all. If you watch the reactions of people when they are listening, you will see how valuable head nods can be. When they are absent, the listener's charm and energy are dramatically diminished.

Ron on Adding "Noddies" to Your Listening Technique

A television reporter once interviewed me in my home. She arrived with a cameraman in tow who took over my office to set his lighting. In the meantime we chatted, and she gave me a sense of what questions she might ask. Then the interview began.

As we talked, I realized that the cameraman was keeping the camera focused only on me and never once on her. I thought, "If this continues, I'll end up being a talking head. It'll be all me and just her voice in the background." That idea didn't please me at all.

When we finished, she proceeded to get the cameraman to film her doing a variety of reactions. I watched curiously and then I asked, "Why did you record your reactions separately?" She replied, "I wanted to do the interview in your office and I couldn't get two cameras, one to be on you and one on me. Now I can add them to the original tape when I'm editing."

I must have looked puzzled, so she continued, "If I can't get both of our reactions, I have no choice but to record them separately." She smiled and said, "We call them 'noddies.'"

I said, "Noddies? But won't they come across as phony?"

She laughed and said, "No, not if they're done well. I can promise you, the viewers won't be bothered by them in the slightest."

Confession: I saw the interview myself and I must say I was surprised at how authentic her "noddies" looked.

Three Ways to Nod

Head nods are strong indicators of how intensely you are listening and what you are thinking and feeling. There are actually three different kinds of head nods—the slow, the faster, and the very fast. Each has its own special meaning and usefulness. Most people will recognize them.

First, there is the very slow head nod, which means, *"I'm following you; I'm thinking about it."* The slow head nod does *not* necessarily mean that you agree.

Second, there is the slightly faster head nod, which says, *"You're right, I agree."*

Third, there is the much faster head nod, which says, *"I agree and I'm excited by what I'm hearing."*

Try them out on your friends and see the results.

Your Tools for Charming Others

Nodding signals to other people that you are warm, friendly, and paying attention. It's an important element of charm. Develop the habit of nodding and acknowledging other people when they are speaking. When you forget to nod and just listen without moving, it can be disconcerting to most speakers.

CHAPTER 14

The Fifth Signal: Whole Body Language

In a conversation, keep in mind that you're more interested in what you have to say than anyone else is.

—ANDREW S. ROONE

W hen you are seated, how you position your body and the way you sit signals the degree of interest you have in a person speaking and what the person is saying. When you lean toward someone, it is as though you are saying with your body, *"I find you fascinating; you are drawing me toward you with a magnetic force."* Leaning away may suggest, *"I'm bored, I can think of a dozen things I'd rather be doing than talking to you."*

Everything Counts

As a rule of thumb, try to keep your whole body turned toward the other person. If you cross your legs, do so with your top leg and knee pointing *toward* the person. Make sure your arms are unfolded and use your hands for emphasis when you speak. In these ways, you create a clear picture of openness and receptivity.

When you're standing, it's important to monitor the distance between you and the other person. To decide how much space is appropriate, check your own reactions when people get too close or too far from you. Then apply what you've learned in positioning yourself with others. If a person tends to inch closer to you, then you were too far away; if the person tends to ease away from you, then you are invading his or her comfort circle.

The Circles of Communication

Imagine three concentric circles, with you as the center point. The first circle is about two feet from you to the other person. This is the personal or intimate space, reserved for romantic partners and family members. If you invade this space as a business or social acquaintance, you will make the other person distinctly uncomfortable. You're reaction is likely to be that the person is trying to intimidate you by getting "in your face."

The second circle is two to six feet away from you and is the space appropriate for social or business acquaintances. When you want to be charming, be sure to stand, sit, and talk within this distance, no closer and no farther away.

The third circle is from eight or ten feet outward. This is the circle of protected distance or safety, used between yourself and strangers. Any sudden movement by someone you don't know from this space into your social space, closer than eight feet, will cause you to become alert and aware.

Ron on Establishing a Comfort Zone

Wild animals are especially careful about keeping their comfort circles intact. When my wife and I visited Namibia, one of the special places to go to was Cape Cross on the Skeleton Coast. We were told that at any given time there are between 250,000 and 350,000 seals basking on the beaches or swimming in the sea.

With the beaches literally carpeted with seals as far as you could see (ignoring the overwhelming stench), it was a fascinating experience to walk among them. As we moved toward them, they moved away. We stopped; they stopped. We moved a couple of paces; they moved a couple of paces. They had a "comfort zone" that had to be observed. The same is true for people: Too close and we intrude, even threaten. Too far and we destroy intimacy.

Speak with Your Body

Whether you are standing or sitting, when you deliberately want to say with your body, *"I think what you are saying is mesmerizing,"* lean in or move slightly closer, but make sure you don't intrude into the comfort circle.

In one very funny episode of *Seinfeld*, Jerry refers to Elaine's latest date as a "close talker." When he talks to anyone, he stands so close that the other person literally bends backward trying to avoid his face being in their face. This kind of person is trying too hard and comes off as aggressive and insensitive.

Your Tools for Charming Others

The next time you're speaking with someone, turn your whole body toward him or her and give the person your complete attention.

If you are sitting, lean toward the person as if you are hanging on every word. Watch the mouth and eyes, gently "flicking" or shifting your gaze from one eye to the other while you are listening. Try leaning slightly forward rather than sitting upright or leaning backward. If you cross your legs, do so with your top leg and knee pointing *toward* the other person.

When you are standing, make sure you are maintaining a comfortable distance between you and the other person. Face the person directly, stand two to four feet away, and shift your weight slightly forward onto the balls of your feet. This movement will be imperceptible to the other person, but he will feel that you are fully engaged with what he is saying. Remind yourself by saying to yourself, "Energy forward!"

Always keep your whole body turned toward the person speaking.

Unfold your arms and use your hands in animated fashion when you speak.

If people are saying something that is important or significant, lean a little farther in. If they say something amusing, relax by sitting or leaning back a little. Then move back in when you want to create more intensity.

All of these signals suggest that you are fascinated by what the people you are talking to are saying. These techniques will make them feel wonderful and they will love you for it.

CHAPTER 15

The Sixth Signal: Body Language to Avoid

Friendship is a strong and habitual inclination in two persons to promote the good and happiness of one another.

—EUSTACE BUDGELL

Just as positive body language dramatically increases your "charm quotient," there are certain body positions that affect people in a negative way. Many poor listeners are guilty of them. You may inadvertently be using these undesirable positions yourself. If so, you will want to avoid these charm-busters in the future.

Poor listeners make the mistake of turning their heads toward a person when they are speaking, but allowing their body to be inclined away from the speaker. This suggests that you don't really care about what the person is saying, but you're pretending that you do.

Poor listeners sit with their legs crossed so that their top leg and knee points away from the speaker, thereby appearing to close themselves off to the message.

Another negative message that destroys any chance of your being charming is when you slump in your chair, as if you want to ooze through the back and get away from the speaker. One of the best ways to counter this negative tendency is to sit up straight and not allow your back to touch the back of the chair.

Often people make the mistake of folding their arms when they are listening. The speaker views this posture as a way of blocking out what she is saying. You can avoid this by making sure that your arms are unfolded and your hands are open, to signal honesty, sincerity, and genuine interest.

Observe the behavior of others. When you see one or more of these negative signals, the listener is telling you at an unconscious level that he is either not interested in what you are saying, or he is completely opposed to it. In personal relationships, especially at home, these contrary signals may indicate that the other person is agitated about something else and cannot pay attention to you until that issue is resolved.

Dr. Albert Mehrabian of UCLA conducted a seminal study of communication some years ago and concluded that, in face-to-face conversation, your body language conveys 55 percent of the message you are sending. Your tone of voice conveys another 38 percent of the message, and the words themselves are responsible for only 7 percent. It is amazing how quickly others read your body language and draw conclusions about you, even if they are incorrect. That's why you must always be conscious of what you are saying by the way you position your body in conversation.

It turns out that women are vastly more sensitive to body language than are men. Research shows that a woman can join a social gathering of fifty couples and assess the state of each of their relationships within about ten minutes of entering the room. A man could spend hours in the same room and have no idea what was happening in the relationships of the other couples.

Ron on Controlling What Your Body Says to Others

I once worked as an image coach with an attorney named Bruce who had been sent to me by his own attorney. It was a high-dollar lawsuit in which Bruce alleged that his new employers had fraudulently misrepresented themselves. He was to be deposed on video by a notably aggressive defense attorney. To check out how he would do on video, his attorney did some role-playing with him and questioned him as though he was actually being deposed. He recorded the result and then played it back. One look and he called me in.

I decided to make my own video. For that purpose, his attorney had supplied me with a list of questions that Bruce might face during questioning. When he arrived, I sat him down and set up my video camera. Then I role-played being the opposing counsel and cross-examined him. Without comment, I just ran through some of the questions to see how he might come across to the jury.

Then I played back the results for him to see. It was a real shock to him.

Bruce was a big, overweight man dressed in expensive but now tight-fitting clothes. There he was on the video monitor, slumped back in his chair, with his straining belly almost popping the buttons off his shirt. He rarely changed his position in any way—he just slumped. Even as we talked he stayed slumped back away from the camera.

I played back my recording and said to him, "Let's be objective; if you were a member of the jury who didn't know this man, how would he come across to you?"

He was far from being a stupid man and tried to be truthful about his personal evaluation. "He looks a little overweight and perhaps a little too sure of himself. I don't think he would make a good impression."

He watched another minute or two of the video and said, "In fact, he would probably make a rather poor impression."

He turned and looked at me and said, "If you were a member of the jury how would he come across to *you?*"

Without hesitating I said, "Fat-cat lawyer, makes a lot of money, smug, arrogant, doesn't give a damn. They're all alike—I'll show *him!*"

The point is that Bruce wasn't necessarily any of those things, but his body language and total demeanor created that impression. And that's how he would be judged. Something needed to be done.

We worked hard on delivery techniques. He lost a little weight (which enabled him to avoid straining his buttoned jacket), sat upright, softened his voice, and even leaned forward now and then as though he was eager to answer their questions. I was delighted to see him change from "The Fat Cat" to "The Gentle Giant." He won his case.

Sometimes people fold their arms or slump, simply because it's comfortable to do so. I know I do. When you're with people you should always be aware of signals that may create a negative impression and immediately change them. When *you* need to connect, when you want to be charming and persuasive, you must be in control of what your body is saying to make sure you are sending out all the right signals.

Your Tools for Charming Others

Be aware of your body language at home and at work. Consciously decide to send a positive message of warmth, concern, and involvement with the way you sit and stand.

Observe the body language of others to see what kind of messages they are sending. Turn down the volume on your television and try to ascertain what the different actors are thinking or saying.

CHAPTER 16

The Seventh Signal: Vocal Reassurances

Friendship redoubleth joys and cutteth griefs in halves.
For there is no man that imparteth his joys to his friend,
but he joyeth the more; and no man that imparteth
his griefs to his friend, but he grieveth the less.

—FRANCIS BACON

You will notice that good, active listeners always make little noises like "Uh-huh," "Aah," "Mmhmm," or other assorted sounds. These are what we like to call "vocal reassurances." They are clear indicators of someone who is paying close attention. They are easily identified and much appreciated by the speaker. They increase your charm quotient.

Your Tools for Charming Others

Make reassuring sounds each time you listen to another person. Allow your instincts to guide you as to when to use them.

Combine your vocal reassurances with good eye contact and head nodding. Together, these signals tell a speaker that you are paying attention and thinking about what she is saying. If the other person starts to become more intense or excited, make your vocal reassurances a little louder to reflect the degree of your interest.

CHAPTER 17

The Eighth Signal: Verbal Reassurances

A friend is a person with whom I may be sincere. Before him, I may think aloud.

—RALPH WALDO EMERSON

Vocal reassurances are essential to charm. But if you combine them with *verbal* reassurances, you double their impact. Eye contact, flicks, body inclines, and head nods and tilts together make a great impression on people—but once you add the power of vocal and verbal commentary, you become a totally charming conversationalist.

The first type of verbal reassurance consists of *noncommittal* words and phrases. They are defined as noncommittal because they don't necessarily mean that you agree with what is being said. Words and phrases such as *"I see,"* *"Really?"* or *"Well, is that so,"* reassure people that you are listening and keeping in step with them, but you remain neutral. Noncommittal words or phrases are used as polite reassurances in general or casual conversation. They fill the air during small talk at cocktail parties and other social events.

When you are prepared to commit yourself and want to agree or support what is being said, you then use words and phrases such as *"Yes, without question,"* or *"I agree, absolutely,"* or *"You hit the nail right on the head,"* and the like. At this time you become an ally in the conversation—you have taken sides. Before you offer such comments that convey agreement, always be sure this is what you want to do.

When processing a person's words, tone of voice also has impact. Have you ever said something to make someone else angry then declared your innocence by saying, "But I only said such and such." Usually the other person responds immediately by saying, "It's not what you said; *it's your tone of voice."*

Your Tools for Charming Others

Introduce vocal and verbal acknowledgments into your everyday conversations, especially when you're on the phone. Use vocal reassurances, or basic sounds, when you don't want to sound too involved or want to remain neutral on a subject. Include more verbals, those specific words of agreement, when you want to show you agree with and support the speaker.

CHAPTER 18

Practice Being Charming with Friends

Treat your friends as you do your pictures,
and place them in their best light.

—JENNIE CHURCHILL

You've heard it said that "practice makes perfect." The truth is that *imperfect* practice makes perfect. You must be willing to make a few mistakes, and feel a bit awkward at times, if you are going to master any skill, especially the skill of charm. The rule is that *anything worth doing well is worth doing poorly at first.*

To develop your charm quotient by bringing all your

communication skills together, you should ask a friend to help you. Think of this person as your sparring partner, with whom you can make mistakes before you get into the actual ring of social and business communication. This type of practice can benefit both of you.

Begin by explaining what you are trying to do. Explain to your friend the importance of the various elements of listening in becoming a charming conversationalist.

During this exercise, your friend should be seated in front of you, as though you are having a cup of coffee together. You are going to try to react to your friend's conversation without talking back—just by listening. Then you'll be asking your partner for feedback on how much you seemed to be involved. Ask your friend to avoid asking questions but rather to talk to you at length, about anything that comes to mind, rather like delivering a monologue.

Also point out, at the very start, that you are serious about learning these listening skills and it would help you a lot if there were no kidding around, no distractions, when practicing this exercise. Here's why.

Ron on Taking Listening Skills Seriously

Several years ago my wife studied to become a Sangoma in KwaZulu-Natal in South Africa. That's the Zulu equivalent of a shaman. Her training was long and arduous and took place over three years. Because we lived in San Diego for six months each year, she was given permission to divide her training into three-month sessions. The sole condition was that I would help her continue her training when she was absent from Africa.

The exercise that we used to train her was similar to

"Twenty Questions," though much more serious. It was designed to teach her to trust her senses and intuition so that she could "see" with her mind's eye.

The similarity to the parlor game nonetheless struck some weird part of my funny bone. I began by asking, "Is it bigger than a bread box?" Nicky laughed and said, "That's funny, but please stop horsing around."

Taking no heed I then said, "Is it smaller than a breadbox?" I should have known better. I have never experienced a room where the temperature dropped so radically and rapidly. Talk about being frosted. But I learned this lesson: If you agree to help another person practice something remember that if it's serious for one, it should be serious for both of you.

Your Tools for Charming Others

With a friend, practice eye contact, eye flicks, head tilts, body inclines, head nods, and vocal and verbal reassurances. Try them one at a time, in stages (e.g., first, eye contact, flicks, and head nods and tilts; second, vocal and verbal reassurances; third, body inclines).

You may have to arrange a few practice sessions to run through each technique thoroughly, but once you feel you've got the hang of them individually, you can put them all together.

After three or four minutes, stop and ask your helper questions such as:

Did I appear to be really listening?

Did I seem to be "in the moment"?

Did you feel as though I cared about what you were talking about?

Did I seem totally involved with you?

If the response is less than enthusiastic, try again until you get the hang of it. Eventually you will hone your ability to be an attentive listener and you'll have it for life. You will be able to make each person you meet feel good about him or herself, and feeling good is what charm is all about.

CHAPTER 19

Be Careful
with Advice

The propensity to give advice is universal. But don't worry;
the propensity to ignore it is also universal.

—BRIAN TRACY

I n Chapter 18 you practiced an exercise where you had to react to a friend's conversation without talking back—just by listening. Now let's bring home another point about how to practice attentive listening.

Ron on Being a Patient Listener

Many years ago, my wife and I were at home having dinner. She obviously had faced a pretty heavy day at the office and was uptight about the day's events. She began to tell me about the ins-and-outs of a problem she was having with a member of her staff. She began quite calmly but soon developed a high head of steam. As she spoke, her anger seemed to feed on itself and she became more and more incensed.

Unfortunately, I wasn't really watching or listening to her. My brain was busy with the answer to her problem that had just popped into my head and, unfortunately, straight out of my mouth. "Look, if you had given her the opportunity to correct her mistake, maybe..."

She interrupted me, "What are you talking about? *Are you saying it was my fault?*"

"Well, no, I was only ..." That was as far as I got.

"Who asked you?" she yelled. "Who asked you? All I wanted you to do was to listen and nod your head a couple of times."

"But I only wanted to help."

"You can help by keeping your opinions to yourself and listening," she said. "I don't want any advice when I'm so angry. Nobody wants advice when they're that angry!"

She was right—*nobody* does!

The moral of this story is that no matter how good you think you've become in displaying charming behavior, being a *patient* listener is the glue that holds all your skills together. Your attentive silence at the appropriate time demonstrates your interest, patience, and caring.

Your Tools for Charming Others

The next time someone comes to you with a problem or difficult choice, turn it around and ask, "What do you think you should do?" And then listen patiently without interrupting.

If a woman asks a man for his opinion about what to wear, she has usually made up her own mind already and is just seeking confirmation. You have a 50 percent chance of being wrong.

Instead, you ask her, "Which outfit do you think looks the best?" Whatever her answer, you agree and say, "That's the one I was going to choose." You'll sound like a genius, and charming as well.

CHAPTER 20

The Power of Patient Listening

People are always willing to follow advice
when it accords with their own wishes.

—LADY BLESSINGTON

Before you stop listening and start speaking, always take the time to consider what's going on with the person or people you're speaking with—that is, their emotional level. No matter how many ideas or insights may occur to you, if the other person is excited or angry or unhappy, it's *still* listening time for you.

Be patient. Give them a chance to let off steam. When they are ready, they'll ask for your opinion and, if they're looking for answers, they'll ask questions. Sometimes a person's emotions and the listener's logic are like oil and water—very difficult to mix.

Your Tools for Charming Others

Whenever you are "attentively listening" and the person speaking seems to be very emotional, listen with added patience before you say anything. Let the person talk and get all of his or her anger or emotion out before you attempt to jump in and offer any suggestions.

Most important, be careful about giving advice unless someone asks for it. Your sympathetic listening will be much appreciated.

CHAPTER 21

Be Quick to Smile and Laugh

Against the assault of laughter nothing can stand.

—MARK TWAIN

There's no question that smiling and laughing are clear indicators of how much you are enjoying being with someone. When the occasion and the subject allow it, always be quick to smile and laugh.

A genuine smile involves the muscles that surround your mouth and your eyes. When you smile, make sure you get all of your face to smile. Let it go right up to your eyes.

Now I don't mean grinning like the Cheshire Cat at everything that's being said, or laughing at every mediocre quip or joke. Overdoing it could raise suspicions that you're being phony or too openly trying to curry favor.

Remember also that smiles that appear genuine don't "switch off" abruptly. Real smiles seem to linger for a moment or two. A smile that doesn't linger really isn't a smile.

There are very good psychological reasons to allow yourself to smile and laugh easily and naturally. Here is an illustration.

Ron on How Humor Is Contagious

In my early days as a theater director, the very first comedy I directed was *Come Blow Your Horn* by Neil Simon. It was a grand Broadway hit loaded with funny lines and a delightfully entertaining cast of characters in amusing situations.

When the cast and I got together to read through the play for the first time, we all slapped our thighs, held our ribs, cackled, howled, and generally reveled over Neil Simon's wizardry. During rehearsals and as the days went by, we all laughed less and less.

A few days before opening night we completed a run-through of the performance. It went smoothly and was word perfect, but it was flat. Nobody in the cast, including me, chuckled, tittered, or even cracked a smile. It was like we were doing Ibsen rather than Simon. I sat there wondering what had been so funny in the first place.

Opening night there was a full house of dignitaries, critics, and well-turned-out theatergoers. I sat in my usual place in the back row on the aisle (so I could leave in a hurry if the audience turned ugly—just kidding) and have never been so anxious. The lights dimmed, the curtain went up, and the play began. Within minutes, the audience began to laugh and laugh and laugh, and what was most interesting—I was laughing, too! How come? It was the same stuff that I'd heard during three weeks of rehearsal and that I'd quit finding funny, and yet here I was laughing again—why?

The answer was *infection*. Smiling and laughing is very infectious. I laughed because they laughed, which refreshed my memory of what I had found so funny before.

I went many times to see that production, my first successful attempt at directing comedy, and I laughed almost as much at every performance I saw.

There's a lesson here for everyone. When you charm, you are being the audience for other people and the infection rule is just as true. When you smile and laugh, others will be inclined to smile and laugh right back at you.

A caveat: Watch out for people who smile with only one side of their mouth turned up. One should be cautious about lopsided smiles—they could be halfhearted or less than honest.

Your Tools for Charming Others

The next time you are in a conversation, wait for the right time to show a smile as the conversation dictates. If the conversation and speaker are serious, you look serious. If the talk is about light, amusing things, encourage yourself to smile.

You don't necessarily have to *agree* with what is being said; you simply have to match the other person's mood. If she is being enthusiastic and you want to charm, allow yourself to smile with her enthusiasm.

CHAPTER 22

Be Quick to Praise

Praise, like gold and diamonds,
owes its value only to its scarcity.

—SAMUEL JOHNSON

We all enjoy recognition, especially if we have accomplished something we think is worthwhile. When people you are with talk about things they are evidently proud of, there is a simple way to intensify their pleasure.

Be quick to praise their wisdom, generosity, thoughtfulness, quickness, cleverness, or whatever is appropriate.

You can be sure they will regard your praise as another indication of your charm.

Appreciation and praise are vitally important to all of us. It is the fuel in the furnace of motivation. Without recognition and praise, many of us would perform well below our potential. Research indicates that many employees respond more positively to praise than to a raise.

Remember when you have seen your child, spouse, a friend, or coworker light up with pleasure because you praised or admired or showed appreciation toward them? Remember how it feels when it happens to you?

Ron on a Critic's Reviews

I can remember as clearly as if it were yesterday my very first major theater review in the newspaper. I was directing a play by Maxim Gorky called *The Lower Depths*, and it was my first professional production. *Depths* is a great classical work but a great challenge to cut your teeth on as a director. Naturally I was flattered at being given the opportunity and frightened by the immense responsibility.

Early the next morning after opening night, I raced out to get the newspapers. I sat in my car for what seemed like an hour before working up the nerve to open them and see if it was thumbs-up or thumbs-down. Then I took the plunge.

I opened the newspaper and with shaking fingers, turned to the theater page. And there it was, the headline: "Great Play Gorky, Great Production Arden." My stomach contracted with pleasure. Then I read what the critic had to say. He saw my faults as well as my virtues and for him, the virtues obviously had outweighed the faults.

I was at the beginning of my career as a director and his carefully weighed praise contributed considerably to my motivation, momentum, and pleasure. That's what praise can do, and people rarely get enough of it.

Yours Tool for Charming Others

One of the best definitions of self-esteem is how much a person considers herself or himself to be *praiseworthy*. The more you genuinely praise people's behavior, the more they like and respect themselves, and the better they feel toward you. To be most effective in giving praise, you should follow these guidelines.

First, be *specific*. The more specific the praise, the greater impact it has on the person's feelings, and the more likely it is to motivate the person to perform even better in that area in the future. Instead of saying, "You're a great secretary," you should say, "You did a wonderful job on that proposal and getting it out so quickly yesterday."

Second, praise *immediately*. The faster you praise people after they have done something praiseworthy, the better they feel and the more likely they are to repeat the action.

Third, praise for both large and *small* accomplishments. As Ken Blanchard says in *The One Minute Manager*, "catch them doing something right."

Praising others for their accomplishments is something most of us do not do often enough. *You* must be the exception to the rule. Praise makes people feel wonderful about themselves and is a key element of charm.

CHAPTER 23

Use the "Act as If" Principle

The best way to create a feeling, if you have it not,
is to act on every occasion where that feeling is desirable
as if you had it already, and you soon will have.

—ARISTOTLE

In 1905, William James of Harvard University, the father of American psychology, made a remarkable observation. He said that the best way to experience an emotion, if you don't actually feel it, is to *pretend* as if you already feel it until it becomes a reality.

The repeated actions of enthusiasm soon generate the real feelings of enthusiasm. If you *behave* as though you are happy or excited, you will soon begin to *feel* happy or excited. Your outward behavior will create the corresponding inner feeling.

You Can Control Your Actions

Psychologists have found that it is difficult for people to switch their emotions off and on at will. Emotions are not under the direct control of the will.

Your actions, however, are largely under your control from moment to moment. By controlling your actions, you can behave as if you already had the emotions you desire to have, similar to the "outside-in" approach in Chapter 8. So your actions actually help to create those emotions.

Actions Trigger Feelings

The "act as if" principle says that if you act as if you already felt a particular way, your actions will soon trigger the feelings to go with them.

When you meet with another person, act as if that other person is absolutely *fascinating*. Treat the other person like a movie star or Nobel Prize winner. Listen with your full attention. Lean forward and hang on every word. Nod, smile, and acknowledge, giving a continuous series of verbal and vocal assurances. The effect will be electric.

Very often, by using attentive listening techniques, you will be able to bring out the other person's insights and observations, which may amaze you. In no time at all, you will actually find yourself deeply interested in the other person. You will find her to be fascinating, and her words to be intelligent and enjoyable.

Brian on Lessons from a Long Bus Trip

A long time ago, I was forced to take an eight-hour bus ride to get home because of an airline workers strike that had paralyzed all air transport. I found myself sitting next to a scruffy-looking character in jeans, with long hair, who was going to be my seatmate for the entire trip. What could I do?

I decided to try out this "act as if" principle I had just heard about. I turned to him and introduced myself, then asked him where he was from and what he did for a living. It turned out that he lived on a farm but that he had become fascinated with small planes. He had sent away for a kit and built himself a one-seater that he flew around the farm country. Eventually he competed in air shows. He went on to tell me about crashes and near-death experiences, and his recovery from broken legs and accidents.

The more I practiced attentive listening, asking questions and acknowledging his responses, the more fascinating things he told me. To this day, I remember how those eight hours flew by as he regaled me with stories about his life and upbringing.

Ron on Using the Power of Your Mind

I was having coffee with a friend of mine recently and he said, "You're into this sort of thing; maybe you can give me an explanation."

He went on. "A week or so ago, I woke up feeling lousy, so I decided not to go into the office. I just sat around in my bathrobe, didn't shave or shower, watched TV a little, and by midmorning I felt much worse."

I asked, "What did you do? Did you go to see your doctor?"

He shrugged his shoulders. "No, I'm not the doctor type. But, here's the point. The very next day, I got up feeling under the weather again but decided I had too much work to do to stay home. I had an appointment I had already postponed from the day before and other urgent things. Off I went, all suited up, and by midmorning I felt much better! Why was this?"

I said, "It was your attitude that made the difference. It's a perfect example of how attitude can affect us physically. Once, everyone thought the reason you felt better was purely mental, but now we know that it's also biochemical. By engaging in behaviors of being well—showering, shaving, getting dressed and going off to work—you actually change your body chemistry, which then causes you to feel better."

He digested the information for a moment. Then he said, "So it's a combination of the power of the mind and our internal pharmacy department that makes the difference."

Actions Affect Feelings

In the same way, when you become accustomed to practicing the charm techniques described in this book, you not only *appear* to be listening more convincingly but you actually *do* listen more efficiently and remember more effectively. It's as though by getting your body (the "outside") to do the right things, you promote the right attitude (the "inside") and the right chemistry.

By incorporating attentive listening techniques into

your life, the payoff is not only that you *appear* to be an involved and caring listener, but that you can actually *become* an involved and caring listener, which will prove to be much more rewarding for you as well as for the other people in your life!

Your Tools for Charming Others

"Fake it until you make it." The next time you are talking to anyone, in business or socially, *act as if* that other person was absolutely fascinating. Hang on every word. Lean forward with great interest. Pretend for a moment that this person is going to give you a million dollars if he likes you. Act accordingly.

In no time at all, you will find yourself deeply interested in the other person, and by some magical chemistry, this individual will begin to share observations and insights that may surprise and delight you. Many lifelong friendships have started this way.

CHAPTER 24

What You Say and How You Say It

A man's character is revealed by his speech.

—MENANDER

The first step toward becoming a completely charming person is to become a great listener. Sooner or later, though, it will be your turn to *speak*. What you say and how you say it are essential ingredients in your ability to charm and persuade others.

Ron on Speaking with Charm

I have a delightful old friend, Cecil Williams, a successful theater director for many years. I acted in several of his productions. He was without doubt one of the most charming people I've ever met. He epitomized all the elements of charm that we've written about in this book.

What most impressed me about him was the way he turned every word he uttered into a show of support, concern, interest, involvement, and caring. He had plenty of opinions of his own and many strong ones, but they were always communicated with respect—as an exchange of ideas, not as competition.

An Essential Speaking Skill

There are several skills you will need when it is your turn to speak, and they'll be covered over several chapters. Let's start again with eye contact, but from a different angle.

Time magazine once scooped the other media and did the first major interview with Mikhail Gorbachev, the then visiting Russian president. His ability to communicate with power and forcefulness his ideas on economic and political reform was one of the major reasons he ascended to the presidency of the USSR. One of his strongest communication skills was noted by the *Time* reporter who wrote, "The first thing you notice on meeting President Gorbachev are his eyes, their intensity, their directness, and their power."

Few of us use eye contact well. Developing this skill is critical to increasing your ability to charm.

The Way You Look at People

The rules used for eye contact when speaking are different from the rules used when a person is listening. When you're in a one-on-one conversation with another person, look at the other person's eyes no more than 85 percent of the time. Maintaining eye contact all the time creates too much pressure. With that much eye contact, you virtually pin the other person to the wall. Instead of being charming, you come across as too intense.

How do you feel when someone is talking to you and never takes her eyes off you? It can be intimidating and even threatening. Notice the way villains in the movies use that kind of unyielding eye contact when they speak.

When you are speaking in a group, you should shift your gaze from person to person, gently, one person at a time. Use your eye contact to reach out and include people in what you are saying, as if you were *scooping* them into the conversation. Everyone you are talking to should feel the power of your warmth and attention.

Your Tools for Charming Others

Make a point of practicing good eye contact with anyone you talk to. Be sure you don't overdo it—look at the other person's eyes no more than 75 percent to 85 percent of the time, otherwise you risk becoming overbearing. Look deep into the person's eyes rather than superficially. It's a definitive way of saying, "I see *you!*"

The Look-Aside

Speech is a mirror of the soul; as a man speaks, so is he.
—PUBLIUS SYRUS

When you are the one doing the talking, the *look-aside* is a powerful communication technique. It is a casual glance to one side or the other of the listener's head, when you momentarily redirect your focus from the person's eyes to the side of the face.

Look-asides should be done casually and intermittently. Never look *above* the listener's head, because that will convince the listener that there's something or someone distracting you. Frequent looks *below* the listeners' eyes will lead them to believe they might have food on their face or gravy on their clothes. Look-asides are not meant to give you the opportunity to look at other things or people;

rather, they are there to release the listener from too much intensity coming from you. In one-on-one conversations, they are essential.

Your Tools for Charming Others

The next time you're speaking with someone for any period of time, practice shifting your gaze to his right or left ear, and then back to his mouth and eyes.

Make sure your look-asides are short, never for more than two or three seconds; otherwise you will look distracted. Remember that your objective is to maintain good eye contact without making the other person uncomfortable.

The Art of Speaking Slowly

Think before you speak, pronounce not imperfectly,
nor bring out your words too hastily, but orderly and distinctly.
—GEORGE WASHINGTON

Many people, because of excitement or nervousness, speak too fast and listen too little. People who speak too fast can be both frustrating and irritating.

Have you ever been stuck in a traffic jam simply because you didn't have enough time to understand what the traffic reporter on the radio said? Near *what* off-ramp was that accident, and what was the alternative route? If only these reporters didn't speak so fast. They are professionals. Don't they *know* it's difficult to absorb a lot of information so quickly? If they would simply slow down, you'd have time to grasp the situation and make the decision to take an alternative route.

Have you ever received a message on your answering machine where the return telephone number was spoken so rapidly or incoherently that you couldn't get the last four numbers? You end up having to replay the message, sometimes more than once, to get the right number.

Give People Time to Think

We all know people who fast talk and are difficult to listen to. You could even be one of them. The trouble with fast talk is that it invariably creates negative impressions and virtually no positive ones. A fast talker gives you no time to think. What kind of person comes to mind when you think of a fast talker? Don't you think of a used-car salesman, a con artist, or someone who is trying to manipulate or hustle you into something that is not in your best interest?

Fast talk makes a speaker sound less thoughtful and more self-centered, which affects how sincerely and honestly that person comes across. Such speakers seem interested only in what they have to say. Fast talk is a sure way to neutralize any opportunity for charm.

Better Speaking Using the Slow-Down Technique

What is the solution for fast talk? There are two techniques you can use. The first, covered here, is simply to *slow down*. The second (covered in Chapter 27) is for you to learn how to use *silences* in conversation.

If you been told many times that you speak too quickly, there's an internal monitor you can use to control speaking too fast; it's called your *comfort zone.* Just as we have comfort zones on the outside, where standing too close to someone is intrusive and too far away destroys intimacy, we have comfort zones inside, too.

When you're doing something unfamiliar or out of the ordinary, you will often feel decidedly uncomfortable. You will have an almost irresistible urge to go back to doing it the old way, even if the old way was not working all that well.

We are all creatures of habit. We too easily slip into a rut and then resist all pressure to get out of it. We are always more comfortable doing things the way we have become accustomed to doing them. It's like the ritual we go through when we get ready for the day. First, the left shoe, then the right, then lace the right one, then the left. If you try to change the pattern, it feels odd.

A Simple Experiment

In our seminars, we often ask people to fold their arms and notice which arm is on top. Then we ask them to *refold* their arms with the *other* arm on top. Try it yourself. Doesn't it feel odd? This is the same feeling you have when you attempt to change an old habit.

But all growth and personal development comes from forcing ourselves out of our comfort zones into the zone of *discomfort.* If we never challenge our comfort zones we will never change—and that includes changing for the better.

Old habits die hard, and rapid speaking is among the most persistent of them. If it's a habit you are having trouble kicking, the very least you should do is make sure you slow down when you are making your more important points. This technique alone will create the perception that you are speaking more slowly overall.

It is important that you keep practicing at speaking more slowly. After a while, you'll start to develop a new comfort zone at your new pace of speaking. You will then feel uncomfortable when you speak too quickly because the new, slower speed is becoming more and more comfortable for you. And what's more important, you'll find it's much more comfortable for your listeners, too.

Your Tools for Charming Others

Here are two exercises you can use to stretch yourself out of your comfort zone and into the performance zone of higher achievement.

First, get a tape recorder and tape yourself reading aloud. Speak at a speed that sounds uncomfortably *slow* to you. Your instinct may demand that you speak at your old speed, but pay no attention to it. Now, play back the recording. You will soon discover that although you sounded slow to yourself when you spoke, it will sound just right on the recording. You can check this out by asking a friend or family member to listen to your recording.

Second, use the same technique during a conversation with a friend. Though the tempo may still feel too slow to you, it will almost certainly be fine for the listener.

Remember, in the early stages of learning to slow your speech, you will and *must* feel uncomfortable. If not, then you're probably still speaking at your old, quick speed.

CHAPTER 27

The Eloquence
of Silence

He who does not understand your silence
will probably not understand your words.

—ELBERT HUBBARD

I n the early days of his presidency, George W. Bush was judged to be a rather poor speaker. Sometimes it was almost painful to watch his bungled attempts to get his message across in his prepared speeches. Something happened along the way that improved his ability to speak more effectively. His aides hired some of the top speechwriters in the business. But in addition to better speech material, there was something else. He learned to speak with greater clarity and impact by using pauses, even if they were used too often at times. The change was significant and approval ratings for his speech delivery rose.

Pausing gives a person time to think, to keep control of the content, and it gives the audience a chance to relate to what's being said. You can become a better speaker simply by pausing for a second or two at various intervals during your delivery.

It is during the *silences* that your listeners will have the chance to reflect on what you say. They are able to picture in their minds what you are talking about. They have the opportunity to weigh your meaning, to connect and respond to your feelings.

In addition, pauses allow listeners to have an inner dialogue with you. They actually talk in their heads expressing their inner thoughts. As a listener, haven't you often found yourself saying things in your head like, *"I disagree,"* or *"What a good idea,"* or *"I read something about that,"* etc.? The more inner dialogue you inspire, the stronger your connection with your listeners will be.

Here is an important secret about the art of speaking well: You can't go wrong with silence. Even if you don't always pick the ideal place for a silence, your listener won't know the difference—he will be too involved with you and what you are saying. In a conversation, nobody thinks, *"Now, wait a minute, that pause was in the wrong place."*

Your Tools for Charming Others

Practice pausing at the end of a thought, or just after having made a key point. This technique helps a listener to know where one thought ends and another begins.

Remember to pause especially after you've said something important, complicated, or unusual. Let the listener digest what you've said while giving yourself time to think and to breathe.

CHAPTER 28

Excessive Fillers Are Charm Killers

*The poor speak very fast, with quick movements,
to attract attention. The rich move slowly and
they speak slowly; they don't need to get your attention
because they've already got it.*

—MICHAEL CAINE

Inexperienced, unprepared, or nervous speakers often fill their sentences with sounds such as *aah, umm, uh,* and *er.* They're known as fillers. Fillers are a way of creating the space to give us time to think. We use them in an attempt to hold onto the listener's attention while we're trying to find the right thoughts and words. Your fillers are saying, *"Don't stop listening, I haven't finished yet, just hang on."*

It can be terribly irritating when somebody "umms" and "ers" their way through a conversation. You may begin to get a knot in the pit of your stomach or your mind may be saying, "For heaven's sake, get on with it!" Unless you have a particular desire to cling to these peculiar and incomprehensible noises, get rid of them. Nobody likes to hear them; fillers are charm-busters.

Your Tools for Charming Others

The best way to eliminate fillers is to slow down your speaking style and *deliberately* use more silences. It is as simple as that: If you use silences, fillers disappear. Whatever you do, don't be overly self-conscious in trying to avoid fillers. You don't know where and when they're going to happen. Trying to anticipate an unconscious act could drive you crazy.

Instead, concentrate on using silences every time you feel an "er" or "umm" emerging from your lips. Incorporate silences into your everyday conversations, especially whenever you realize that you are speaking too quickly, and the fillers will take care of themselves.

CHAPTER 29

Charming People with Your Voice

*Any man may speak truly; but to speak with order, wisely,
and competently, of that, few men are capable.*

—MONTAIGNE

The sound of your voice has a profound influence on the mood and receptivity of the person you are talking to. The mere tone of your voice accounts for 38 percent of your message (as noted previously, body language and the words themselves are responsible for the rest).

Who would you prefer to listen to? Someone with a high, shrill voice that pierces your ears and makes you wish you were somewhere else, or someone who is able to charm you with a warm, full voice that makes you feel as though you're being wrapped in a cashmere blanket? It's no contest. Cashmere wins every time.

What about monotonous and boring voices? "Blah" voices, we call them. They are sure to reduce both the attention and the receptivity of the listener. You have to use your voice the way storytellers do, with animation and color that makes whatever you talk about—even if it's just the weather or the stock market—sound interesting. Resolve to be a storyteller rather than a talking fax machine.

Lower Your Voice

When you want to sound close, friendly, warm, reassuring, intimate, or caring when you speak, keep your voice in the lower range where the deeper sounds are. The lower to middle tones are also great when you want to reason with the other person or show that you care or are being thoughtful.

Also, remind yourself to slow down. It's very difficult to be close, friendly, warm, or thoughtful when you're speaking too quickly. Most of us tend to slow down naturally when expressing our deeper emotions.

Try this: Say quickly, *"I'm deeply concerned about you; you mean a lot to me."*

Now, try it more slowly. It will sound much more sincere and real.

Pick Up the Tempo

On the other hand, if you have a flat voice, push yourself out of your comfort zone and pick up the tempo when you want to sound excited or energized. Use the upper sounds of your voice, but not too high. Vary your speed and tone. Choose your pace and tone based on what you're talking about and the mood you want to create.

Deeper vocal sounds suggest size and strength; higher sounds convey smallness and weakness. If you hear a deep barking behind a door, you don't expect to see a Chihuahua; if you hear high-pitched barking you don't expect to see a Great Dane. Powerful people deliberately speak more slowly and with lower tones.

New Voice, New Career

There was a prominent football player who was about six feet seven inches tall and weighed about 280 pounds. He was a great player, but though he was a giant on the field, in everyday life he had the voice of a Chihuahua—very incongruous. With coaching he learned to change the way he used his voice. This new deeper voice changed his life. He ultimately left football and became a successful sports commentator on television.

Your Tools for Charming Others

First, select an interesting chapter or article from a book or magazine that is easy to read and speak. Then read this material into a tape recorder at a leisurely pace. Gently lower your voice toward the deeper, warmer tones that you can comfortably reach. Don't force it. Let it come naturally, varying your tone up and down. Repeat this exercise until you are pleased with the result.

Second, play this pleasant-sounding voice of yours over and over again at home and in your car. As your new voice imprints itself on your subconscious, you will find yourself speaking in that same tone of voice in your everyday conversations.

When you use the deeper sounds more frequently, the overall perception your listener forms is that of a richer and warmer voice, and a more charming personality.

CHAPTER 30

Be a Charming Conversationalist

Sir Arthur Conan Doyle is said to have once left a dinner party raving about Oscar Wilde's gift as a conversationalist. "But you did all the talking," his companion pointed out. "Exactly!" Conan Doyle said.

—STEPHEN FRY

Your charm quotient is entirely determined by the way you look, listen, and speak to people. But there is an additional quality that those who have charm enjoy— they are great conversationalists.

Being a focused and patient listener is essential to charm. Using a pleasant voice and not talking fast also raise your charm quotient. Another key to being charming is to be sensitive to what others want and *don't* want to talk about.

If the people you're speaking with want to unload their feelings or just talk about trivia, let them. It is true that there are those who will go on forever about things that are unimportant or boring to you. And it's hard to be charming when you are being bored out of your gourd. Some people will talk endlessly about their problems and their personal lives. You don't want to be impolite, so what can you do?

Usually you have two choices: One is changing the subject 180 degrees, the other is trying to grin and bear it. But when you've decided that enough is enough, there is another choice for the true charmer. You can use a well-placed question.

For example, a 180-degree change would be if you were to take over the conversation and switch abruptly to another topic. If someone is pouring out her heart about a pet dog, you suddenly start talking about your interest in intergalactic travel. A better way is to do a twenty or thirty degree shift and slip in a comment about your own appreciation of dogs. Then you might parlay into a question about dog shows—"What did you think of the best-in-show pick at Westminster Kennel Club this year?"—or performing dogs, dogs for the blind, rescue dogs, or some titbit about pets and vets.

Your Tools for Charming Others

In your next conversation with a friend or colleague, look for an opening to change the subject obliquely, into a *slightly* different direction, twenty or thirty degrees off center, so the change of conversation is almost imperceptible. Try interjecting a well-placed question.

While you may not be able to change the subject entirely, you'll have charmed someone by keeping the conversation meaningful to that person. It's a wonderful opportunity to be creative while focusing on someone else's needs instead of your own. Making others feel special is one of the keys to becoming a disarmingly charming person.

CHAPTER 31

Steer the Conversation

*The true spirit of conversation consists more
in bringing out the cleverness of others
than in showing a great deal of it yourself.*

—LA BRUYÈRE

The purpose of steering the conversation is not to dominate it (that would be the *opposite* of charm), but to make sure that, with your support, it continues to go in the direction the other person wishes so that his or her interest and involvement are constantly engaged.

Imagine yourself in a social situation. You're standing there alone, minding your own business, with a plate of snacks in one hand and a glass of wine in the other. Out of the blue, somebody launches at you and immediately starts talking about himself: *"I do this; I did that."*

In ten seconds flat, you're thinking, *"How can I get out of here!"* Now, let's imagine the same situation, only this time somebody comes over to you and in ten seconds flat has *you* talking about *yourself.* Who would you prefer to spend time with? There's no contest.

Talk About What the Other Person Cares About

All of us enjoy talking about the topics we're interested in—especially when the listener seems to enjoy it, too. When people discuss a topic that's important to them, they tend to reveal a great deal about themselves to sympathetic listeners. They show their likes and dislikes, their preferences, beliefs, and ideas. When you are the listener in a conversation, you must listen closely to discover the various paths you can take in steering the conversation. What you're looking for is a way to keep up your end of the conversation while encouraging others to take over as much of the conversation as they like.

An added bonus is that you can often learn as much from people with whom you have little in common as those with whom you agree. An open mind is a receptive mind, and it creates the endearing manner of the charming person.

Your Tools for Charming Others

The surest way to steer any conversation is to ask questions that begin with *who, what, why, when, where,* and *how.* Any question that starts with one of these words cannot be answered with a yes or no. The response requires facts, figures, feelings, and details. And the person who asks these questions has *control*.

One of the most powerful ways to elicit reactions, responses, and opinions is to ask the questions, "How do you feel about that?" or "What do you think about that?" whenever a story or anecdote is told. These questions almost always elicit a more extensive answer, and the person speaking will think that you are both charming and intelligent, just for asking.

CHAPTER 32

Do Your Homework

Knowledge is pleasure as well as power.

—FRANCIS BACON

Anytime you are getting together with someone, socially or professionally, whom you particularly want to impress, do your homework. Learn what you can about that person *before* you actually meet. It's the best way to be charming and interesting to others. As Dale Carnegie once said, "You can make more friends in a day by being interested in others than you could in a year by trying to get them to be interested in you."

A Good Investment

The higher the value you place on a relationship, the more time you should invest in learning about the person before you meet. Find out as much as you can about her or his likes and dislikes, hobbies, educational background, business interests, and social activities. Armed with this information, you can lead the conversation in many different directions that you know the person will enjoy. The idea is to know more about these people than they know about you.

Brian on the Value of Preparation

Some years ago, I was building a national sales organization. I soon discovered that it was easier to take over an existing branch than it was to set up offices, recruit salespeople, and train from scratch. I learned of a successful business owner with a crack sales team who was discontented with the company he was representing. I decided to recruit him and all his people for my business.

In asking around, I discovered that he was heavily into numerology and made all his decisions based on the numbers of the birth dates of potential business partners, as well as the days of the month and week. I got a couple of books on numerology, read up on the significance of particular numbers, and then arranged to meet with him on the best day of the month, numerically speaking.

One of his first questions of me was my birthday. I was prepared. I told him that it was a certain day, month, and year that added up to a "lucky number" for business relationships. At the end of the meeting, he joined my organization and went on to be a highly productive member of my network. The preparation was the key.

Seek First to Understand

Sometimes it's not possible to obtain information, especially if you're meeting someone for the first time. In this type of situation, you must be completely focused on the other person.

When you first meet, talk about yourself as little as possible. There's a wise old saying: "You never learn anything when you're talking."

Think about that. You can't talk and listen to people at the same time. It is only when *they* talk and *you* listen that you will learn anything about them. If they seem reluctant to open the conversation, you take over with the intention of getting them to talk as soon as possible.

You can begin by talking about what's current or prominent in the news (avoid politics or religion until you know more about them), or by making reference to a recent hit movie or popular television program, books, sports, or fashion. If you've mentioned a movie, ask them what they have seen lately. Ask what kind of movies they prefer, and so on.

Find a Subject of Interest

Here's an example of how you can piggyback on what another person is talking about. Suppose the other person says, "I'm so frustrated by the way people drive nowadays. There's no consideration for anyone else. Nobody has patience anymore; they just want to get to wherever they're going as fast as they can and you'd better get out of the way."

Let's analyze the possibilities in this simple statement. It's safe to say that this person has a bee in his bonnet about something—but what? About driving in general? Perhaps.

About inconsiderate behavior? Maybe. About other people's lack of patience? Possibly. There are three different directions you could take the conversation safely. You could reply with, "I agree," and then proceed to briefly talk about an incident that happened to you. That approach is particularly useful if the other person seems to be running out of conversation.

Always remember that the more you can learn about other people during a conversational exchange, the greater will be your potential influence on them. The more and better questions you can ask that piggyback on their background and interests, the more they will find you to be charming.

Your Tools for Charming Others

Remember, *the person who asks questions has control.* There are three powerful questions you can ask of any new acquaintance that will enable you to control the conversation and appear charming at the same time.

First, you ask, "What sort of work do you do?" Most people are deeply interested in their work. It plays a central role in their lives and is a major source of their identity. They love to talk about it and describe what they do to others.

Then, when they have told you what they do, you ask, with great interest and curiosity, "How did you get into that line of work, anyway?"

This question will invariably be answered with all kinds of details about the person's history, experiences, and background, all explained in the form of a life story. Sometimes the story can go on indefinitely. People usually feel that the story of their careers to this point is one of the most fascinating stories ever told.

The speaker may slow down periodically to determine if you are really interested or if you are just being polite. Whenever he pauses in his story, you ask, "And then what did you do?"

He will immediately expand on his last comment and continue telling you more of his story. Whenever he slows, ask "And then what did you do?" He will be completely charmed by you.

You can ask other, similar questions as well. "Tell me more about that." "How did you feel?" "And what did they do?" "What happened next?"

If you like, you can introduce your own thoughts. When you do say something about yourself, resist the temptation to become too talkative. To pass the ball back to the other person, end your comment about yourself with another question to get the other person talking again.

CHAPTER 33

Keep the Ball in Their Court

*The chief ends of conversation are to inform or
to be informed, to please or to persuade.*

—BENJAMIN FRANKLIN

Charming people keep up their end of the conversation by passing the ball back and forth easily and naturally.

Your goal is to participate actively in the conversation while at the same time encouraging your conversational counterparts to take over as much as they want. You are like a tennis player who concentrates on keeping the ball in play. Like a tennis coach, you hit the ball so your student can reach it and get an opportunity to hit it back. The longer the rally lasts, the more valuable it is for the student, as well as for the conversationalist.

Reading Each Other

Most conversations begin with polite, social banter. These light exchanges allow both parties to gauge the mood and receptivity of the other person. You can then shift the conversation to more profound matters, depending on the direction you want to go.

One of the best ways to keep the conversational ball in play is to use questions that spin off from what you're already talking about. For example, imagine that at the beginning of the conversation you began talking about food.

You say, "Have you tasted these snacks? They're delicious!"

The other person replies and then you speak again, introducing a new question: "I must say, my enjoyment of food always threatens my waistline. What type of foods do you prefer?"

Whatever the answer, you agree. "Me, too," you say. "I love most foods as long as they're well prepared and tasty. Do you eat out a lot?"

The other person gives an answer, then you continue: "I think the best home-cooking-type restaurant in town is [name your favorite restaurant]."

That comment leads into the next question: "Have you ever been there?"

The person answers, and then you continue. "You must try it. Just about everything they make is exceptional. Do you have any restaurants that you particularly enjoy?"

For each answer, you continue with a follow-up question: "Do you enjoy eating out?" And so on.

Obviously, the conversation could go in a hundred different directions but, as you can see, the basic idea is to keep the conversation bouncing back to the other person. It is not complicated or difficult to do. It just involves putting your ego on the back burner and attending to the needs or interests of the other person. It is the key to being charming.

Your Tools for Charming Others

In conversation, remember that it is not about *you*. It is about the other people around you. Most people are so concerned about themselves and the impression they are making, they lose their naturalness and spontaneity.

When you talk to another person, forget about yourself. Don't worry about being liked or popular. Instead, focus on making others feel liked and popular.

Don't
"Kill the Ball"

*The success of the actions of great men depends more upon
the purity of their hearts than upon the means of their actions.*

—VEDAS

To "kill the ball" is a tennis term. It's what you do
when your opponent is out of position. You pounce
on the ball and hit it so hard that you win the point.

When you and another person are having an argument,
that is what you generally try to do. You try to find a point
of fact or position where you can win without your opponent being able to respond.

But, when you are trying to be charming, it is utter

madness to try to stake out a winning position. The last thing you want is for the conversation to fall "out of charm" because you are beginning to find yourself in disagreement with the other person. Then you are in the potentially dangerous position of wanting to kill the ball and with it, all your efforts so far.

Brian on Trying Too Hard to Impress

When I was a young firebrand, I got involved in politics at a time when the state was convulsed with political acrimony. I spent hours studying and reviewing every possible fact on the key issues of the day. I wrote letters to the editor that were published regularly in the major newspapers, and was regularly featured as a guest on the controversial radio shows. I really knew my stuff.

I would argue, debate, and overwhelm anyone who wanted to discuss the issues of the day. I was like a verbal Zorro, slashing skillfully at any opponent, and even at my friends. Then one evening, I was at social gathering with a lot of prominent people. When I arrived, they were gathered in groups talking and bantering back and forth.

Knowing I could dominate and win any political conversation, I walked up to a group of businesspeople I knew and began speaking about something in the day's news. As I opened my mouth, as if on cue, the four men glanced at me and then dispersed quickly in four different directions, leaving me standing there by myself. It was a lesson I never forgot, and I never again attempted to use my verbal prowess to dominate a conversation.

Do You Want to Be Happy or Right?

No matter how strongly you feel or how ridiculous you think other people's ideas may be, avoid even the tiniest sense of conflict. Conflict in a conversation is a certain charm-buster. That doesn't mean you can't be firm in your opinions, but don't let the idea of winning the point overwhelm your true purpose—which is to be warm, genial, likable, and a pleasure to be around. In a word: to be *charming*.

Your Tools for Charming Others

First, be clear about your intent in any conversation: It is to be charming. It is not to win the point or to impress others with your cleverness.

Second, avoid conflict at all costs. It is an immediate charm-buster. It's difficult to be perceived as being charming when there is even a semblance of hostility in the air.

Third, you may be pleasantly firm with your opinions, but don't try to kill the ball. Present your point of view gently, tentatively, and then let it go. Don't become so involved in being "right" that your charm is obscured in a cloud of argument.

Finally, only take over the conversation when other people make it clear that they want to hear from you. When they ask a lot of questions about you, that means they are most likely interested in you. Oblige them, but don't risk becoming a bore by going on too long.

When it comes to charm or winning the point, if you win—you lose!

CHAPTER 35

Get in Step with the Other Person

What lies behind us and what lies before us
are tiny matters compared to what lies within us.
—ORISON SWETT MARDEN

Timing is everything in getting through to people, especially in the area of charm. As it says in Ecclesiastes, "There is a time for every purpose under heaven." Your job is to determine when it is.

Have you ever tried to talk with others only to find yourself out of step with their mood? You're cool and mellow; they're agitated and uptight. You're feeling life's a ball; they're down in the dumps.

The two of you are worlds apart and any attempt to

make a connection fails. You may try to be supportive and reassuring, but nothing seems to work. You just can't connect. Why is that? It could be because, at that moment, the two of you have different rhythms and are moving at different speeds, like automobile gears grinding.

It is the same with people. You have to find a way to mesh gears, to make sure that you and the other person are in sync, so that no matter how different you are, you can create rapport.

Practice Mirroring and Matching

Long before the advent of neurolinguistic programming (NLP), professionals used an acting exercise called "mirroring and matching" to learn what it was like to be a leader or follower. The exercise trained actors to work in harmony with each other by synchronizing their movements or behaviors. For example, one person would make up a tune and hum it, and the other would try to hum the same tune seemingly at the identical time. Two people would, with each other's cooperation, become a mirror image of each other.

Most of us have the latent ability to adapt to different types of people but, for all kinds of reasons, we don't. Can you imagine what it would be like if you could only relate to people *exactly* like you? How narrow your world would become. It's the reason many people become so inflexible and judgmental. If you don't do it the way I do it, if you don't see the world exactly as I see it, then you're wrong, unworthy, irrelevant.

People with charm avoid being inflexible and judgmental. They enjoy seeing the world through others' eyes as well as their own. That is one of the most fundamental secrets of charm—*being able to see the world through the other person's eyes.*

Your Tools for Charming Others

The next time you are in a conversation, try this exercise. First, consciously mirror and match the other person or people with whom you are conversing by listening to their speech and watching their body language. If they speak rapidly, you match them. If they speak fairly slowly, you do the same. If they gesture a great deal, so should you. If they are restrained in their gestures, you be the same.

Second, whatever seems to be their topic of the day, try to see it from their point of view. Nod, smile, agree, and offer reassurances. The idea is to get them to say in their minds, "I am very comfortable with this person. We have so much in common. We are very similar." We all tend to like and feel at ease with people who seem in tune and in harmony with us. We find them charming.

CHAPTER 36

Practice Makes Perfect

What we learn to do, we learn by doing.

—ARISTOTLE

Practice your new charm skills whenever you can. When you first learn new techniques, they may feel a little awkward. This is normal. It is only when you repeat these charm skills in conversations with real people that you learn them to the point where they become second nature.

It is not enough that the players on a football team work out and learn and practice the plays. It's the experience they get, game after game, that allows them to develop conditioned reflexes.

Make These Skills Automatic

As you practice and repeat these techniques, you will automatically program the behaviors of being charming into your subconscious mind. It will then take over and these techniques will happen naturally and easily. That's been our goal from the beginning.

You've seen the concentration and effort in a baby learning to walk, or a child learning to ride a bicycle, or an adult learning to play golf or square dance. Pure, dogmatic, do-it-by-the-numbers repetition allows us to do many things without having to think about them.

When you boot up a computer, certain programs automatically come into operation. If there were no programs already installed in the computer's memory, just like they are installed in your subconscious, then you'd have a blank screen and a blank mind.

Your Tools for Charming Others

Practice every skill you've learned so far on every occasion. Focus on one skill at a time. Use the skills of charm with your family, friends, new acquaintances, and people you work with during the day. Practice will give you the experience and confidence you need to be charming in almost every human interaction.

Treat each person you meet like a million-dollar customer, like the most important person in the world. When you approach people this way, you will make them feel wonderful about themselves. They will find you completely charming.

CHAPTER 37

Translate Skill into Art

Do you see a man skillful in his work? He will stand before kings.

—PROVERBS 22:29

Once you have all the techniques needed to create charm, there are some personal commitments that can only come from you. It is when these attitudes are added to your listening, looking, and speaking abilities that your well-practiced techniques rise above themselves and become the "art" of charm.

Your Tools for Charming Others

Blend all your abilities together into the *art* of charm by incorporating these attitudes into your listening and speaking habits. These are the commitments that will bring pleasure to you and others:

- Resolve to be pleasant and pleasing with each person you meet.

- Resolve to be gracious and understanding, no matter what is going on.

- Resolve to be caring, considerate, and nonjudgmental.

- Resolve to be quick to smile and quick to praise.

Paradoxically, it is only when you put the other person ahead of you that you end up ahead yourself.

CHAPTER 38

Now You Have to Do It!

*There is no substitute for talent. Industry and
all the virtues are of no avail.*

—ALDOUS HUXLEY

A wrestling coach told one of his athletes, "You have real talent and you work hard and that's great. However, if you want to be a top wrestler, you need lots of experience." If you want to be a top athlete, working out is not experience, conditioning is not experience, and training is not experience. They are what they are—no more. The coach was saying that only by going out there and wrestling competitively would this athlete gain experience.

The same thought applies to nearly everything we do. Thinking about it isn't doing it. Getting ready isn't doing it.

Practicing it isn't doing it. Visualizing it isn't doing it. *Doing it is doing it!* There's no other way. To get all the seams ironed out so that you can act effortlessly and naturally, you have to do something over and over again under real-life circumstances until you don't need to think about it anymore. The secret to performing at your best is to condition your mind so thoroughly that your behaviors and responses are easy and automatic.

You have to do a lot of charming.

Your Tools for Charming Others

Visualize yourself in a social or business situation, and see yourself as relaxed, genial, warm, friendly, and charming. Imagine you are exerting your charm on another person and they are smiling and enjoying your company.

Affirm and repeat to yourself regularly, "I am a completely charming person." Every time you say these words, create a mental image of yourself charming another person and enjoying it.

Finally, to program your subconscious mind with the elements of charm, continually "act as if" you are a world-class charmer. Resolve to walk, talk, gesture, and smile exactly as if you already exert a magnetic influence on everyone with whom you come in contact. Allow your conditioned reflexes to guide the way. You don't have to "make" it happen, you *let* it happen. You have already begun to experience the power of charm. Now you have to believe in your charm and enjoy it.

Always stay "in the moment." For a charming person, the only time is now. There's no "next time," no "tomorrow," no "I'll try again." You can only be charming when you are fully focused on the other person and nothing else. As Ram Dass said, "Be here now!"

Roll Out
the Charm

*Half the world is composed of people who have
something to say and can't, and the other half who have
nothing to say and keep on saying it.*

—ROBERT FROST

Your ability to charm others will be like the cherry on the parfait, socially, and money in the bank, professionally. Think of the enormous value your newly acquired charm will have in your social world. You will make new friends easily, be the person everyone would like to talk to at a party, delight your friends and family, and charm the pants off total strangers.

The Key to Advancement

In the business world, can you imagine the advantages your charm skills will give you? You will make more sales to customers who are eager to buy from you. You will negotiate more effectively, buying at lower prices and selling at higher prices.

Your company will make you the key person to meet important business contacts. Your colleagues and superiors will look forward to spending time with you because they value you not just for your intelligence but for your charm as well.

You will be paid more and promoted faster. Your personal and market value will be higher than you could ever have expected before. People who can help you will open doors for you, and opportunities to advance will increase.

Now it is all up to you. You have nothing to lose and everything to gain. Who doesn't enjoy being with someone who seems to appreciate them, cares about them, listens to them, responds to them—who makes them feel important and treasured? Who doesn't like to spend time with a charming person?

Don't you?

The Power of Charm on the Telephone

Many of us spend vast amounts of time on the telephone. With the advent of cell phones, more people are chattering away in any and every place you can imagine. The development of telephone charm can dramatically increase your effectiveness in dealing with other people. Try these simple techniques.

Step 1: The First Impression

You know the old saying, "You never get a second chance to make a first impression." Often that first impression isn't created face-to-face but on the telephone.

Many sales professionals and businesspeople never actually meet their customers in person; they do business solely on the phone. They are successful with this technique because they develop telephone personalities that come across charmingly and persuasively.

A Common Experience

True story: A customer called up an appliance company and a woman's voice answered abruptly, "K and B." The caller said, "I beg your pardon," and she again said "K and B" in the same grim, totally charmless manner. The caller paused and then asked gently, "Why didn't you say good morning?"

There was silence. Then the caller said, "You have such a nice speaking voice, I would love to have heard you say good morning." Still silence. "Could you say it now?" Another silence and then, finally, "Good morning."

The effect was striking. By now her voice and manner were totally friendly; there was, in fact, a smile in her voice. The customer responded by saying, "That was terrific— thank you." The customer's impression of the receptionist, and the company she represented, changed radically from her first "K and B" to her last "Good morning."

What a little thing to do, to smile, and what a difference it makes. Don't forget, a smile can be heard and felt in your voice on the phone. The listener might not smile, but *you must!*

Step 2: Looking for Clues to How Someone Speaks and Listens

The beginning of a telephone conversation gives you a great opportunity to discover how the person on the other end of the line communicates. You will soon discover whether their conversation is dominated either by what the person *thinks* about things or how he or she *feels* about things. Psychologists call them cues, *systematic* cues and *heuristic* cues, respectively. We call them *clues*.

The words people choose and the way they sound as they speak are clues to what is important to them at that time. When you talk and listen to other people, be prepared to synchronize with whatever communication mode they are using and respond with more of the same.

Details versus Emotions

For example: When someone seems particularly interested in discussing the informational details of a topic, you should avoid talking about feelings and emotions. The reverse is also true. If the other person seems to be emotionally involved with the subject you are discussing, avoid talking about practical and logistical things until the person changes course. You don't want to be talking past one another; you want to be on the same wavelength.

Imagine the disconnect there would be if a friend or family member was talking about the beauty of the mountains and how peaceful it is to vacation there (heuristic-based response) and you insist on discussing the geology of the region and the type of crops grown there (systematic-based response). You might as well have just arrived from Mars!

Others talk about feelings and emotions; you talk about facts and figures. The result—disenchantment! They talk about numbers and logistics; you talk about mood and emotions. The result—calamity!

Step 3: Giving People What They Want

If you want to be charming, remember this point: It's not about you. Forget about yourself. Oblige the other person.

When you are talking to someone on the phone, treat the mouthpiece of the phone as though it is the ear of the person you are talking to. Speak warmly and gently. Caress it with your voice. It will help make what you say sound more intimate, caring, and personal.

Here now are the twenty-two most powerful ideas ever to help you become more charming on the telephone:

1. *Encourage the other person to talk.* When it's your turn to talk, don't go into a series of mini-monologues. Instead, ask questions and listen closely to the answers. The more you listen, the more charming you sound.

2. *Speak clearly, simply, and directly.* If the other person uses ordinary language without complicated words, you must do the same. Nothing can create a barrier more rapidly than sounding superior by using ten-dollar words. Keep away from any language that cuts the other person out of the loop.

3. *Listen attentively, because it's the only way you can learn.* Most people would rather talk than listen, especially on the phone. Resist this tendency, and when the other person wants to talk, focus on listening.

4. *Be a patient listener.* Although you may be ready with an answer after the first few words they say, allow them to complete their thoughts and air their feelings until it is your turn to speak.

5. *Be an active listener.* Use vocal and verbal acknowledgments and reassurances such as, "Uh-huh," "Yes, I see," "Mmmm," "Really," "You don't say," "Of course," and the like. These simple remarks let the other person know that you are fully engaged.

6. *Interrupt without offending.* Interrupting can be read as a negation of what a person is saying and thinking—it's a small put-down. If you absolutely must interrupt, always take the blame. Say something like, "Forgive me for interrupting, but I didn't want to forget this point."

7. *Use short, graphic examples and stories.* Dry is deadly. When it's your turn to speak, create a little theater with your comments. It wasn't just "a sunny day," it was "a warm, glad-to-be-alive, sunny day." Be colorful and pictorial.

8. *Never assume—never presume.* No matter how friendly the conversation is, never stretch the familiarity level above what the other person has set—especially when it comes to kidding around. If you can't say it to your mother or father, don't say it to someone else.

9. *Don't rush.* Slow down and use the deeper sounds of your voice. Slower and deeper is much more attractive in speech than faster and higher.

10. *Use pauses.* When you or the person you are addressing needs time to think, try introducing a pause. Warn the other person by saying, "Take a moment to consider that," or, "Give me a moment to think." When you pause, don't take too long or you'll get a *"Hello, are you there?"*

11. *Don't oversell information.* Give people the information they need—no more. Some people will balk at making decisions or coming to conclusions if they are overwhelmed. Don't tell them what they don't want or need to know. Be alert to the fact that your overenthusiasm could overfill their interest level.

12. *Be empathetic to people's moods and concerns.* If they're unhappy, be unhappy for them; if they're glad, be glad for them. If you are trying to sell people on a product or an idea, remember that once they see you as a friend who cares about them, they will be more open to changing their minds or opinions.

13. *Keep your voice animated and energized.* Vary the volume of your voice and the speed of your words. Slow down on the more important comments; soften your more confidential remarks. Speed up with details and unimportant information. Nothing is more boring and demotivating than a flat, monotonous voice. It is more powerful than a sleeping pill.

14. *Express your emotions.* Your voice and manner should project enthusiasm, concern, excitement, and pleasure. You want to convey the intensity—even the passion—of your convictions. But take care not to overdo it, because then you're overselling.

15. *Smile into the phone.* A smile can be both heard and felt. It changes the shape of your mouth, which affects the tone of your voice. Your voice will sound warmer and friendlier if you smile when you are speaking.

16. *Give people what you want from them.* If you want them to be excited, you must sound excited. If you want them to be convinced, you must sound convinced. They won't give you what you don't give them.

17. *Focus on talking about what is of interest to the other person.* Make sure her ideas, opinions, and concerns are always foremost in the conversation.

18. *Resist giving advice.* This applies on the phone and when speaking with someone in person as well. If a person asks for advice, resist the temptation to respond. Instead ask, "What do you think you should do?"

19. *Always ask permission.* When they haven't asked for advice, but you know they need it, try saying, "May I make a suggestion?" Always be gentle.

20. *Respond to anger or an aggressive manner with gentleness.* If you respond in like manner, you may win the emotional battle but you will surely lose the charm war. Remember that a soft answer turns away wrath.

21. *Don't stop being charming before you've hung up.* Be sure your charm extends into everything you say, including good-byes. Have you ever spoken to someone on the phone who abruptly cuts off the conversation? It makes you wonder if the person meant anything he said, doesn't it?

22. *Think of yourself as mentoring your listener.* Try to be like the best mentor you can remember—informed, patient, kind, caring, concerned, warm, supportive, and protective. Strive to be genuinely helpful and friendly.

Your Tools for Charming Others

Resolve today to become an excellent and charming communicator on the phone. First, keep these suggestions on a single piece of paper and have them in front of you whenever you are speaking on the phone. Review them casually as you speak and look for opportunities to apply them.

Second, treat each phone call as an important meeting with a special client. Get rid of all distractions and concentrate single-mindedly on the voice of the other person.

With a little thought and practice, these skills will become invaluable in your social life and priceless in your business and career; in fact, they will do as much to improve the quality of your relationships as anything else you do.

acceptance, 12–13
achievements, of men, 27–28
acknowledgment, 37
actions
    "act as if" principle, 78–82, 126
    importance of behavior,
        31–34
admiration, 14
advice, 67–69, 134
affirmations, 126
aggression, responding to, 134
Algren, Nelson, 22
anger, responding to, 134
animation, of voice, 98–99, 133
appreciation, 13, 75–77
approval, 13–14
Arden, Ron, 5–7
Aristotle, 78, 121
attention, 14, 17, 35–37
attitude
    "act as if" principle and,
        78–82, 126
    impact of, 80–81

Bacon, Francis, 59, 107

Bernhardt, Sarah, 1
Berold, Ivan, 5–7
Blanchard, Ken, 77
body language
    comfort zones and, 51–53
    controlling, 56–58
    head nods in, 47–49, 79
    head tilts in, 44–46
    leaning away, 50, 52
    leaning forward, 50, 52, 79
    in listening, 44–50
    negative, 54–58
    sitting, 51, 52, 55
    standing, 51, 52
    whole body, 50–53
Budgell, Eustace, 54
Bush, George W., 92
business space, 51

Caine, Michael, 95
Carnegie, Dale, 16, 107
charm
    advancement and, 128
    applications of, 5–7
    art of, 123–124

commitment to, 123–124
impact of, 8–10
from inside out (American
    approach), 31
men and, 19–20, 26–29
nature of, 3–4
from outside in (European
    approach), 31–34
secret of, 12–15
women and, 19–20, 22–25, 56
see also conversation;
    listening; speaking;
    telephone conversations
Churchill, Jennie, 63
Clinton, Bill, 3, 34
Coghan, Stanley, 39
comfort zones, 51–53, 89–91
compliments, 14
conflict, 117
control
  of body language, 56–58
  in conversation, 102–103,
    105–106, 110–111, 113, 116
conversation, 101–122
  conflict in, 117
  getting in step in, 118–120
  impressing others in, 24–25,
    116
  "killing the ball" in, 115–117
  mirroring and matching in,
    119–120
  practicing, 121–122, 126
  preparation for, 107–111
  questions in, 102–103,
    105–106, 110–111, 113,
    131

reading each other in,
    113–114
steering, 104–106
subject of, 102–103, 109–110
see also listening; speaking;
    telephone conversations
crossing legs/arms, 55, 58

dogs, head tilts of, 44–45

Emerson, Ralph Waldo, 61
Emotional Intelligence
    (Goleman), 16–17
empathy, 16–17, 36, 133
endorphins, 18
energy, of voice, 98–99, 133
examples, using, 133
eye contact
  flicking and, 41–43
  in listening to others, 38–43
  look-aside and, 86–87
  in speaking to others, 84–87

familiarity level, 132
fast talkers, 88–89
feelings
  actions in triggering, 79–82
  details versus, 131
  expressing, 133
fillers, excessive, 95–96
flicking eyes, 41–43
Franklin, Benjamin, 112–114
friends, practicing with, 63–66,
    121–122

Frost, Robert, 127
Fry, Stephen, 101

Gardner, Howard, 17
Goleman, Daniel, 16–17
Gorbachev, Mikhail, 84
Gorky, Maxim, 76–77
Greville, Fulke, 35

habits, changing, 90–91
head nods, 47–49, 79
head tilts, 44–46
heuristic cues, 131
Holtz, Lou, 11
Hubbard, Elbert, 92
humor, 72–74
Huxley, Aldous, 125

impressing others, 24–25, 116
infection rule, 73–74
interruptions
    avoiding, 17, 18, 23
    gentle, 132
intimate space, 51

James, William, 78
Johnson, Samuel, 47, 75

laughing, 72–74
Lincoln, Abraham, 14
listening
    attention in, 35–37
    body language in, 44–50
    in conversation, 109

eye contact in, 38–43
genuine versus phony, 42
head nods in, 47–49, 79
head tilts in, 44–46
impact of, 6, 9, 16–21
keys to effective, 17–19
men and, 19–20, 26–29
patience and, 68, 70–71, 132
practicing, 63–66
in telephone conversations,
    131–133
women and, 19–20, 23–24
look-aside, 86–87

Marden, Orison Swett, 118
matching, in conversation,
    119–120
Mehrabian, Albert, 55–56
men
    charming a man, 26–29
    listening and, 19–20, 26–29
Menander, 83
mirroring, in conversation,
    119–120
Montaigne, 97
Morrow, Lance, 30

neurolinguistic programming
    (NLP), 119
nodding, 47–49, 79
noncommital words and
    phrases, 61–62

openness, 51
overselling information, 133

paraphrasing, 19
patient listening, 68, 70–71, 132
pauses, 18, 92–94, 96, 132–133
Perot, Ross, 43
personal space, 51
Plato, 26
pleasure, for others, 6–7, 9
power
    of charm, 9
    of patient listening, 68,
        70–71, 132
praise, 13–14, 27–28, 75–77
promotions, 128
protected space, 51–52
Publius Syrus, 86

questions
    for clarification, 18–19
    in conversation, 102–103,
        105–106, 110–111, 113, 132
    for women, 24–25

reassurances, 37
    verbal, 61–62, 79, 132
    vocal, 59–60, 79, 132
receptivity, 51
reputation, importance of, 2
Roone, Andrew S., 50

St. John, Seymour, 3
Sanborn, Mark, 3, 34
Seinfeld (TV program), 52
self-esteem
    building others', 12–14, 18,
        27–28

at core of personality, 11–12
    of women, 23
self-improvement arena, 31
silence, 18, 92–94, 96, 132–133
Simon, Neil, 73–74
slumping, 55, 57, 58
smiling, 12–13, 72–74, 79, 130,
    133
social intelligence, 1–2, 16–17
social space, 51
speaking
    excessive fillers in, 95–96
    eye contact in, 84–87
    pauses in, 18, 92–94, 96,
        132–133
    tempo of, 88–91, 98–99, 132
    voice quality and, 97–100,
        133
    see also conversation;
        telephone conversations
stories, telling, 132
systematic cues, 131

telephone conversations,
    129–134
    clues in, 130–131
    first impressions, 129
    giving others what they want,
        131–134
"thank you," saying, 13, 75–77
Thokoza, 8
tone of voice, 55–56, 62
Twain, Mark, 72

unconditional positive regard,
    12–13

verbal reassurances, 61–62, 79,
    133
visualization, 126
voice
    quality of, 97–100, 133
    tone of, 55–56, 62
    vocal reassurances, 59–60, 79,
        132

Washington, George, 88
Williams, Cecil, 84
women
    body language and, 56
    charming a woman, 22–25
    listening and, 19–20, 23–24

Zeno of Athens, 41

Brian Tracy is one of America's top business speakers, a bestselling author, and one of the leading consultants and trainers on personal and professional development in the world today. He addresses 250,000 people each year on subjects ranging from Personal Success and Leadership to Managerial Effectiveness, Creativity, and Sales. He has written more than thirty books and has produced more than 300 audio and video learning programs. Much of Brian's work has been translated into other languages and is being used in thirty-five countries. He is coauthor, with Campbell Fraser, of the Advanced Coaching and Mentoring Program and the Coaching Excellence Program.

Brian has consulted with more than 1000 companies—IBM, McDonnell Douglas, and The Million Dollar Round Table among them—and has trained more than 2,000,000 people personally. His ideas are proven, practical, and fastacting. His readers, seminar participants, and coaching clients learn a series of techniques and strategies that they can use immediately to get better results in their lives and careers.

Ron Arden is British born and educated and is widely recognized as one of the leading speech coaches in the world. He devoted many years of his distinguished career to acting and directing, and as a professor of theater arts in the U.S. and overseas, and then applied his extensive theatrical experience to improving presentation skills in the business world.

Designated the "Guru of Speaker's Coaches" for his unique coaching style and his work with many of the world's top professional speakers and members of the National Speakers Association, Ron has been featured in *Time* magazine and has earned wide recognition and numerous awards, among them the Maurice Mascaraenhas Award for Outstanding Resource, the William Soroka Exceptional Leader Award, the Executive Committee Worldwide's Two Hundred Award, and the "We Believe in Miracles Award" from P.A.R.T.S.

Ron is in private practice in San Diego and conducts seminars and workshops throughout the U.S., Canada, and South Africa. His clients include corporations; city, state, and federal agencies; politicians; attorneys; executives; and radio and television personalities.

Brian Tracy University

Brian Tracy has recently founded and is president of Brian Tracy University of Business and Entrepreneurship, committed to helping individuals to achieve financial success and independence as business owners (www.briantracyu.com).

The University offers practical, fast-acting instruction on Business Building, Increasing Your Profits, Getting Started in Your Own Business, Successful Selling, High Performance Leadership, and Maximum Performance.

Using the technology of the Internet, you can learn the essential skills of marketing and sales, production and distribution, advertising and promotion, and how to get the money you need. With BTU, this information is available to you anytime, anywhere.

For a free business assessment, visit www.briantracyu.com today, and get started on the road to riches.